The Freezer Cooking Manual

from 30 Day Gourmet

A Month of Meals Made Easy

30 Day Gourmet Press

Nanci Slagle

Brownsburg, Indiana

PO Box 272
Brownsburg IN 46112

Email: office@30daygourmet.com
Website: www.30daygourmet.com

Photography by Nexis Technical Services
Editorial Assistance by Tara Wohlenhaus, Tammy Davis, Carol Santee, Curtis Dicken

Cover photo credits:
Easy-Reach refrigerator/freezer courtesy of Amana and Maytag Corporation
Shopping photo courtesy of Marsh Supermarkets, Indianapolis, Indiana

Library of Congress Catalog Card Number: 99-095247

Slagle, Nanci
      The Freezer Cooking Manual from 30 Day Gourmet: A Month of Meals Made Easy /
      Nanci Slagle. – Brownsburg, IN: 30 Day Gourmet Press, ©2004.

ISBN: 0-9664467-5-5
1. Cookery   2. Title

Printed and bound in the United States of America

We have the #1 Freezer Cooking site on the web!

- **Access our Members Only section for worksheets & lots more recipes:**
    - user name: recipes
    - password: macaroni
- **Recipes, Recipes, Recipes!**
- **Message Boards filled with:**
    - Tips and info
    - Reader recipes
    - Freezer cooking chatter
- **Shopping cart with great products for your freezer cooking!**

What others are saying about the 30 Day Gourmet plan:

Cooks, Parents & Families say:

The best part about 30 Day Gourmet cooking is how much my husband brags about our full freezer to all of our friends. As a working mom, this has been a godsend. My kids love the recipes.

teacher from Iowa

Although we are a small family, I was glad to see that is not a problem because your system isn't just geared to "large" families. This is a true FAMILY cookbook. Thank you for easy-to-read instructions and ingredients I can pronounce.

dual career family from New York

Just awesome! I'm a whole new person come 6 pm.

home school mom from Florida

After researching all the "once-a-month" cooking books out there, yours is BY FAR the most complete, organized and thorough program we have found.

cooking couple from Indiana

My 18 year old son and I made several meals for him to put in single serving sizes and take to his college apartment. He finds this to be a quick and easy way to have home-cooked meals.

working mom from Ohio

My friend and I are having a great time with this. Our husbands are proud of us and our kids aren't hungry anymore. We're not running through the drive-thru or making a meal out of soccer field food. Thank you for inspiring us! It's well worth it and we're hooked.

busy mom from Missouri

Penny Pinchers say:

This cookbook is the best money I have ever invested!

frugal family from Washington

I recently compared my budget from a "before 30 Day Gourmet" year to an "after 30 Day Gourmet" year. What a surprise! I had cut our grocery spending by almost $1000!!! Thanks for the wonderful book!

computer analyst from California

Great book! It's the only way I cook anymore! I just love the recipes. No one can believe they have been pulled out of the freezer and I am saving LOTS of money!

daycare provider from Virginia

Seniors & Singles say:

Your method works well for retirees who do not want to spend every day thinking of what to cook when we have more fun things to do. The 6 person meal gives us 3 meals in the freezer. I have enjoyed your recipes so much and tell everyone who will listen about this method of cooking!

retired secretary from Texas

As a single person, freezer cooking has been great for me! Making it all ahead and packaging it in single-serving sizes has saved me so much time and money.

aerobics instructor from Nevada

I just started my daughter-in-law in freezer cooking and she loves it! I had been cooking this way for years but your cooking manual made it easier to teach her how to do it.

active grandma from Michigan

Table of Contents

Table of Contents

Dear friends,

Congratulations on your decision to try (at least once more!!) to organize your cooking. Only those of us who have sung those dinnertime blues know the anxiety created by this one little "task".

Do you find yourself "stressing out" every day just about dinnertime? Does your family equate "home-cooked meal" with a visit to Grandma's? Is your grocery basket filled with frozen convenience foods? Are you spending more money on dinner than you want to?

The FREEZER COOKING MANUAL from 30 Day Gourmet could change your life!

Next week your dinner menus could be filled with home cooked foods that you actually look forward to eating! Wonderful main dishes, salads, vegetables and side dishes, and desserts can come from your freezer. These prepared and frozen foods are so delicious and convenient that you will not want to go back to your old methods of meal planning. You'll find yourself saving money (sometimes without even trying!) and you may even notice the stress levels in your home dropping.

When I discovered freezer cooking ten years ago, I had been married for 14 years and was the mother of four children ages 8, 5, 3 and 1 month. I was also a "crisis cook" who didn't think about dinner until the last possible moment. We ate fast food dinners. We ate cereal dinners. We ate my husband's "breakfast for supper" specials. And we ate a lot of hot dogs and boxed macaroni and cheese dinners. Sound familiar?

In my early days of freezer cooking, I tackled the then-daunting task with my good friend, Tara. Together, through trial and more than a few errors, we figured this thing out. In the beginning, we got together once a month and assembled 25-30 entrées for each of us. After a few years, we began cooking every three months. Our 2-day cooking marathons netted us each about 75 freezer meals. As our family sizes, schedules and tastes changed, we found that the "system" we had developed was adaptable enough to "flex" along with us.

This manual is the result of those years of learning along with the input of thousands of freezer cooks who have adopted these methods. 30 Day Gourmet's step-by-step freezer cooking plan has been taught in hundreds of seminars and featured on national television and radio. Our website is the leading source of freezer cooking information and recipes on the web.

Cooking the 30 Day Gourmet way is worth whatever it takes to make it work for you. Nothing beats the relief and great sense of accomplishment you feel when you can take an entrée out of the freezer, go to the zoo or your office for the day, and come home to a 10 minute preparation time for dinner. Now even on the crazy days, you can still enjoy a great homemade meal.

This is a hands-on manual. Make several copies of the worksheet pages as you'll use these each month or access them in the Members Only section of our website. Order one of our Cook's Assistant Notebooks and begin building your own freezer recipe collection. Give it a try and see what happens. I'm guessing that it will make your meals more convenient, tastier, less expensive, lots more relaxing, and even enjoyable! Have fun and please let me know how it goes!

Feel free to contact me by e-mail at office@30daygourmet.com or through our our website at www.30daygourmet.com. I want you to be as successful as possible! If you have cooking questions, a story to share, or a recipe to contribute, I would love to hear from you!

To your success,

Nanci Slagle

Rewards of Freezer Cooking

The rewards of freezer cooking are numerous and each cook's #1 may be different but here are the ones I hear over and over:

It's flexible and fits my lifestyle.
Face it. Our lives these days are busy. I finally figured out that it's unrealistic to think that I can meet the dinner challenge the same way that my mother and grandmother did. Mom always knew by 9 a.m. every morning what we were having for dinner that night. She was busy too, but her day centered around preparing that evening meal. Not at my house! With three teenagers, a sociable 10-year-old and a husband with an erratic work schedule, it's the proverbial revolving door around here. I usually don't know until 4 p.m. who will even be eating with us but that's okay. I can still put together a great meal – all from my freezer. That's just my story, though. Seniors and singles. Work-outside-the-home moms and work-at-home moms. Grandmas, teachers, accountants, even truck drivers! This works for everybody!

It saves me $$$$$.
Eating out or going to the grocery store today for tonight's dinner can be very costly. A family of 4 can easily spend $20+ on a fast food dinner or pre-packaged frozen dinners. Using the Freezer Cooking Manual will lower your food bills! Our cooks average no more than $5.00 for each main dish recipe (4-6 servings) and many spend even less. Think of what you could save! And tell me you don't have a better place to spend that money.

It's healthier.
By using the principles and recipes found in the Freezer Cooking Manual, you will naturally eat fewer processed foods, fats, salt, and preservatives because you are in control of the ingredients in each recipe. You can easily boost your fiber, vitamin and mineral intake by planning ahead and freezing your foods! Substitutions are a snap which makes cooking for special diets much easier when you freezer cook.

I love the fresh, home-cooked taste.
You'll eat few "pre-packaged" and even fewer "drive-thru" foods. Will you miss them? Don't worry about losing flavor. Learning to package your freezer foods correctly takes care of that. There's no skimping on taste at 30 Day Gourmet!

I'm enjoying a greater variety of foods.
Even good cooks run out of time, energy, and creativity at the end of a long day. At 6 p.m. most of us can only think of 2 or 3 entrées we know how to make! Not anymore! With a little planning, 30 Day Gourmet cooks freeze a wide variety of great-tasting foods. American favorites, Chinese, Mexican, Italian – it's your choice!

I have more free time.
With foods ready in the freezer, you will suddenly find yourself with more time at the end of the day. Sure, getting them into the freezer will take some time but those last minute trips to the store, unwanted dinners out and sinks full of pots, pans and cookware are time-wasters of the past.

I have enough to share with others.
Charity and hospitality seem to be lost arts today. By assembling foods in advance, it's easy to take dinner to the neighbor who is ill, a friend who just had a baby, or the family that recently moved in across the street. By cooking multiples of the same recipe, it's also easy to take another entrée out of the freezer for company or to accommodate unexpected guests.

I actually enjoy cooking now.
For many of us, it's not the cooking that we hate. It's the daily grind of it all. Having food in the freezer gives you the flexibility to decide when (if ever) you want to cook. Some use their creative juices for baking great desserts, some for fresh salads and others for trying out new recipes.

Frequently Asked Questions

My Schedule is too busy now. How can I take a whole day just to cook?

The great thing about our system is its flexibility. Don't have a whole day? Do a 3-4 hour mini-session. Or triple up on your dinners for a few weeks and build up some reserves. Cook 10 of the same recipe and find 9 friends who will do the same. Then swap 'em out. There are lots of ways to get the job done! And after you try **The Freezer Cooking Manual** plan, you will realize that the time you save in meal preparation and cleanup each evening is well worth the time it takes to shop and cook in large quantities – even a whole day's worth.

Do I have to be a good cook to do this?

Absolutely not! Only the most basic cooking knowledge is needed for most of these recipes. Our 5 Simple Steps are just that – simple. All of our recipes give very detailed instructions so that even the least experienced cooks can be successful.

Do I need to buy a freezer?

Actually, about 30 main entrèes to serve 4-6 adults each WILL fit into a standard refrigerator's freezer (see cover photo). But it does help to have some extra space. Chest freezers are an inexpensive option and hold a lot more food than you think! Upright freezers are easy to organize and take up less floor space.
As appliances go, freezers are VERY reliable!

How do I come up with the money to get started?

Of course, you realize that you WILL be spending the money on food eventually. Try stocking up on grocery items as you see great sales. After a month or two, you should have most of the ingredients. Have a garage sale, use your Christmas bonus, or earmark that tax return check for some quick cash. Or try just cooking for 2 weeks the first time.

Do I have to spend a lot of money on freezer containers and pans?

Use of freezer bags makes it economical to get started. The foods in them can be thawed and put into your favorite dish for baking. Slowly acquire freezer containers, glass casseroles, and metal baking pans at garage sales and discount stores if you like. Some 30 Day Gourmets use freezer bags almost exclusively, while others opt for a menagerie.

What if I hate to cook?

But you have to eat, right? So do it ONCE in a great while and get it over with. Or try cooking with a partner and make a party out of it!

Will my freezer foods taste fresh?

Having foods in the freezer just gives you the flexibility to decide WHEN you want to cook or bake "from scratch". You'll find that you have more energy now for creative side dishes, desserts, and more extravagant company meals. Our 30 Day Gourmet recipes are made "from scratch". You can choose to pre-bake your entrées and side dishes so that you only have a short heating up period before meals or just pre-assemble your foods and freeze them to cook after thawing. All the aromas and flavors of fresh cooking remain.

How do I know what foods freeze successfully?

Keep reading and we'll tell you! Actually, more things do freeze well than don't.

What if I LIKE cooking every night?

That's great! Open a restaurant and we'll recommend you to all of our readers!

5 Simple Steps
to the Plan

STEP 1:
PLAN IT!

STEP 2:
SHOP! SHOP! SHOP!

STEP 3:
GET READY.

STEP 4:
NOW WE'RE COOKIN'

STEP 5:
STOCK THE FREEZER

Before you Begin

Answer these two questions:

#1 Do I want to cook alone or not?

- What our Cooks Have to Say

- Advantages of Going It Alone

- Advantages of Teaming Up

- Ways to Team Up

- Tips for Teaming Up

#2 What Freezer Cooking method do I want to use?

- What our Cooks Have to Say

- Cooking by Protein Type or the "What's on Sale" Approach

- Cooking by Mini-Sessions

- Cooking BIG!

- Tips for Cooking BIG

Before you Begin

#1 Do I want to cook alone or not?

There are pros and cons to both. Remember too that you can cook alone one time and with a friend the next. The main question should always be: what will be best for me given my situation right now? I know it sounds selfish but don't cook with a friend just because SHE wants to. Maybe that's best for her but maybe you are faster, more frugal and more efficient when you work alone. On the other hand, maybe you will never get this job done without a "cooking buddy".

Sometimes it just helps to hear what other cooks have to say:

Cooking with spouse:

Just wanted to tell you all that I am a newbie who just finished my first cooking session. My unexpected partner was my husband who really likes the concept. A whole day spent together talking and cooking really made it fun. My feet hurt, but the freezer looks so great full of yummy food. We both thought all of the recipes looked so great as they were coming together. We are so excited to have our meals ready to go every day and no more wandering around the grocery store at six 'o clock wondering what to buy. Hope you all are enjoying this as much as I am, what a great idea!!!!!

Carrie

Cooking alone:

When I first read about 30 Day Gourmet I thought that you HAD to cook with a friend. I just knew that wouldn't work for me because of my schedule. I went ahead and tried it alone and it works GREAT! I plan on Wednesday or Thursday, shop on my way home from work Friday and cook on Saturday. My husband takes our daughter "out" for the whole day (dinner included). I turn on the music, wear comfy clothes and shoes and just have a great day to myself. Plus I can put about 50 dinners (there are just 3 of us) into my freezer. What a great feeling!

Missy

I love cooking alone because I can work at my own pace. Sometimes my cooking takes me a few days but that's okay. I'd rather take my time than feel rushed and tied to another person's schedule and tastes. I tried cooking with a friend one time and it drove me nuts. Cooking alone is the way to go!

Sue

Cooking with mom and sis:

The last time my sister and I had a cooking session, it was a disaster. I had always cooked by myself. But my sister recently moved right around the corner, so we decided to cook together, and we added Mom into the mix too. And we decided to cook for 90 days for all 3 families. Well, 3 days later, we were so exhausted. The thought of ever cooking again was just dreaded. The big mistake was not planning well enough. We had too many labor intensive meals to get done. This time, we planned weeks ahead and only cooked for 30 days. We planned what appliances were needed. Mom didn't need any more meals for her freezer, as she still hasn't finished the last session's meals. We studied all the local grocery ads. We went grocery shopping Friday morning. We hit 5 stores in about 4 hours. We spent $189.80 total for 30 days worth of food. That would be $94.90 for each family!!! We started cooking at about 9 a.m. Saturday and finished up at about 7 p.m. This included all the clean-up. Wow! What a difference.

Jennifer

Cooking with daughters:

We just had our first cook day yesterday!! What fun!! My two daughters and I rented a local church kitchen with 3 stoves and 3 sinks and tons of counter space. The $50 charge was SO WORTH IT!!! We started at 7 am and ended at 12:30 in the morning. What a day!!

Diane

Friends cooking together:

We cooked for our second time on Friday and made 60 meals in 7 hours with 5 kids "helping". Thanks for all the great ideas.

Michelle and Lisa

Before you Begin

#1 - Do I want to cook alone or not?

Advantages of Going It Alone:

1. You can set your own schedule.
If you have a crazy schedule, it can be difficult to find a mutually compatible day to cook with a friend or family member. Maybe the thought of putting the kids to bed and then pulling an "all-nighter" cooking session appeals to you! Maybe you need to break up your cook-time over two days. Maybe you really don't know until Thursday what Saturday holds. If that's YOU, cooking alone might be best for you.

2. You don't have to pretend to like "her" recipes.
When you cook with a friend, it can be hard sometimes to agree on the recipes. If she has a "family favorite" that she just knows will freeze well how do you say "I'm sure it's great, but I don't think my family will like it?" That's a tough one. When you cook alone, you are solely responsible for choosing the recipes. You're the only one who knows if you are only freezing homemade chicken nuggets, tacos and hot pockets!

3. You don't have to do any complicated math problems.
Cooking with another person means more math to do. It's as simple as that. To keep everything fair, you have to tally the bills, account for the inventory that each cook brings to the pile of groceries, and resist the urge to pick up extra groceries for your family while you are shopping for both freezer cooks.

4. You can cook and package the food any way you want to. It's all yours!
The actual cooking can be easier too. All of the food in the kitchen is yours. That means that you don't have to measure as carefully when you are dividing up the recipes. You can use a "decide-as-you-go" plan for packaging the foods. If a 9x13 dish is too large for your family, you can pull out all of the smaller ones you have and make them work. Deciding whether to pre-cook your foods or to just pre-assemble them is easier too. Pre-cooking 30 entrèes for two cooks is very time-consuming!

5. You can make allowances for special diets and picky eaters.
If you have someone in your family who requires special ingredients or is a "picky eater", it's easier to allow for that if you cook alone. It can be difficult to find a cooking pal whose family is also lactose intolerant or whose husband won't eat anything but meat and potatoes. Many freezer cooks who have one "special eater" in their family create variations of their regular meals and then freeze them separately for that person.

6. You can quit when you're tired.
Yes, accountability can be a good thing and sometimes it's best to push through and finish. There are other times, however, when enough is enough. If you cook alone, you can pack it up and quit if you choose to. One of our favorite sayings around the Slagle house is "Stuff Happens". And when stuff happens on cooking day (like unexpected guests or a flooded bathroom or a trip to the emergency room or a sick child) it's nice to have the flexibility to just start again the next morning.

7. You can spend time alone without feeling guilty.
Many women who cook alone choose to because they look forward to being alone in their own kitchen for a whole day. If you've never tried it, give it a whirl sometime. I'm a "people person" but I can testify to the thrill of a day alone in the kitchen. I turn on the stereo, stock up on Diet Mt. Dew and have at it. Because I spend most of my days in the office at the computer, it's actually relaxing for me to be in the kitchen cooking. I set the timer every now and then for a 15-minute break, nibble on any parts of my meals that look irresistible, and have a "grand old time".

Before you Begin

#1 - Do I want to cook alone or not?

Advantages of Teaming Up:

1. You can share the planning.
Freezer cooking for the first time can be a daunting task that some people will NEVER try by themselves. It's always easier to tackle a new project with a friend. Two heads usually are better than one and it's no different with freezer cooking. Choosing recipes, tallying your ingredients and planning your shopping may be a lot easier for you if you do it with someone else.

2. You can share the work.
In the long run, it is less time-consuming to cook for two families at once. After all, you are getting out all the same appliances, cookware, and ingredients anyway. Your time-saving comes in making multiples of recipes. It may take 15 minutes to combine the ingredients for one meatloaf but it won't take 90 minutes to do 6 meatloaves. One of you may be especially good at planning and shopping while the other is the cooking expert. Great team!

3. You can share the fun!
Okay, let's admit it. This is the same thing as sharing the work. But why is it that work can seem like fun when there's someone else in the room? Many cooks tell me that they look forward to having a whole day with their friend (mom, sis, neighbor, spouse) more than anything else. And because you're working at the same time, it's a win-win situation!

4. You can share the thrill!
Cooking with someone else means there's another person to get excited about your cooking accomplishments. 30 Day Gourmet cooks have been known to stop for a moment to "ooh" and "ahh" over each completed creation!

5. You can share the cookware.
One very economical reason for cooking with a partner is that each cook doesn't have to purchase every necessary item. Between the two (or more) of you, you will probably come up with plenty of pans, measuring cups, etc. Only one of you needs a food processor or blender, and a mixer. I didn't own much more than an electric can opener when Tara and I began cooking together!

6. You can share the blame.
Something is bound to come up on your planned cooking day that will threaten to keep you from the task at hand. A child's ballgame, a cancelled and rescheduled appointment, a call from the boss - all of these things will seem to be valid reasons for putting it off. If you have promised a friend that you would spend this day in the kitchen, you are less likely to give in to outside demands. The blame game also works if you have botched a recipe!

7. You can share the bounty.
Many people who cook together find it's easy to agree to each give away a certain amount of their food. They have fun choosing a recipient or two. Maybe one cook has a grandmother who would LOVE to have some individual entrées, soups or desserts. Another may have a neighbor with an upcoming surgery who would appreciate an extra meal or two in the freezer. When you plan for these "giveaways" the money that you spend is minimal and it doesn't seem like nearly as much work as it would if you made that meal separately.

Nanci has cooked alone, with friends and with her kids. All great cooking plans!

Before you Begin

#1 Do I Want to Cook Alone or Not?

Ways to Team Up:

Cook with a friend, sister, mom or spouse.
I cooked with Tara for several years and we loved it! When our children were small and we were "stuck in the house" a lot, it was so great to head to her place for our cooking days.

Cooking with a family member can be good because you know each other so well and can be more relaxed about dividing the jobs and the food. Mom can watch the grandbaby and work on the "sit down" jobs. You may do most of the cooking but she has been a huge help and won't take home as much of the food. It's a great deal for both!

Cook with a group in the same location.
It can be a lot of fun to cook with a whole group of people. Some cooks have a house large enough to accommodate 3-5 cooks. Remember that you're not limited to using the kitchen. A dining room with a good-sized table will be great for assembling meals that aren't being pre-cooked. Other cooks have used their church's kitchen or rented a local public building. When you cook in a group, it's fun to work in pairs. One church group paired an older, more experienced cook with a younger, more novice cook. They all had a GREAT day together!

Cook with a group in multiple locations.
We call this "Co-op Cooking". The basic idea is that you get a group of 10 and do a planning session where you assign each cook one recipe that she will make 10 times. The group sets a date a few weeks away to get back together and "swap out" the frozen entrèes. It's much easier and faster to make 10 of the same thing than to make 10 different entrèes. And since you didn't have to assemble the other 9 meals,

it kind of feels like eating out. Per entrée monies are tallied and bills are "evened up" so that everyone pays the same.
(For more info and recipes, check out our Co-op Cuisine eBook at www.30daygourmet.com)

Tips for Teaming Up:

- Don't make a lifelong commitment. Try it once and see how it works. Just because she's nice at playgroup, doesn't mean she will make a perfect cooking partner. And don't just invite the best cook you know. A better question is "who would I love to spend the whole day with?"
- Consider the sizes of your families. It's just easier if the food can be split down the middle. If you have a family of 6 and she has a family of 2, who's going to run out of food faster?
- See if you can agree on 10 recipes. No two families have the exact same tastes but it's easier if you can assemble the same recipes for both of you. If they are a strictly "meat and potatoes" family and yours is a "casserole only" family, you team may not work well.
- Keep careful track of the costs. Consider the cost of the inventory that each person is contributing. Don't shop for groceries that you won't use on cooking day. It's just easier to tally the costs if you limit the ingredients to cooking day only. Of course, mutually agreed-upon snacks and treats are always welcome!
- Split up the recipes by protein type and make enough for everyone. In other words, when each cook assembles a recipe she should be doing hers and the other person's. Your time-saving comes in making multiples.

Before you Begin

#2 What freezer cooking method do I want to use?

When most people hear about freezer cooking they immediately think "cook all day Saturday once a month and get enough dinners to last until the next month". That's certainly one way to get the job done but there are so many more. Again, find a method that works best for you. If using the "what's on sale" method appeals most to you, then go for it. When life is especially busy, the "mini-session method" might be your best bet. If you like to tackle big projects or have a schedule that fluctuates, the "cook big but not often" method may work great for you.

Here's what our cooks have to say:

Mini-Sessions
I want to first tell you that I LOVE the 30 Day Gourmet. I have done two small sessions to get the hang of before I do the full 30 days. I have learned a lot by starting off small. I think I would have given up starting off doing meals for 30 days.

Brenda

I freezer cook by doing 2-3 recipes every weekend and making several of each. I like this way better than doing the whole 30 days. I love that your plan is so flexible and will work for whatever is best for me!

Tammy

Wow! I love 30 Day Gourmet. I'm a full time working mom with two kids going in different direction with their activities and find it very hard to make meals unless they come out of a paper bag. Doubling up on recipes isn't that hard and saves time and money.

Debbie

The beauty of this system is you can adjust it to fit your needs. It doesn't take much longer to make a double, triple or even quadruple batch of something... you eat one, and freeze the rest. Before you know it, your freezer is full.

Sarah

What's-on-Sale
I decide what to cook by what's on sale. I like just tackling one type of meat at a time. Today I zipped into the store and lucked into a sale on chicken thighs - 62 cents a pound. I bought 20 lbs. – I made Crispy Rice Chicken, Parsley Parmesan Chicken, Marinated Chicken and Mom's Chicken Noodle Casserole. All in just a few hours!

Cindy

I usually do "loss leader plans" meaning I base my freezer cooking on what is on sale. When blade roast was on sale, for .99lb, I put six pot roasts in the freezer, with herbs added and directions to add one can of tomato paste, bouillon and water. When hamburger was on sale, I did a hamburger plan with 4 recipes and made 3 of each. So simple.

Teresa

I'm trying to get into the habit of hitting a really good sale at the store and make dishes out of that over the course of a few days or a week, when I have time. Last week my local store had chicken on sale for .49 a pound so I bought six chickens and brought them home and made 4 meals (2 recipes, 2 of each) in no time.

Stephanie

Cook Big
Cooking once a month works great for me. I've been doing it for several years now. In a 6 hour day I can usually get 20 entrées and several sides and desserts in my freezer. It's wonderful.

Vickie

I cook every three months and it's the only way to go! Your software makes my planning easy. The cooking takes 3 days but wow – what a big accomplishment. My friends think I'm some super-cook but it's really not that hard.

Beth

Before you Begin

#2 What freezer cooking method do I want to use?

Three Ways to Freezer Cook

1. Cook by protein-type or the "what's on sale" approach

Lots of freezer cooks use this approach. Rather than planning a cooking day once a month, they wait to see what's on sale and buy up a lot of one meat type. Cooks who follow this plan say that they save lots of money and it's much more manageable. If chicken is on a great sale, they might buy 50 pounds of it. 10 pounds can be boiled and diced for use in casserole-type recipes. 10 pounds can be used in slower cooker recipes. Another 20 pounds can be put into marinade and frozen to cook on the grill. The last 10 pounds can be made into nuggets, patties or other pre-cooked recipes that will make for quick "last minute" meals.

2. Cook in mini-sessions

Cooking in mini-sessions just means that you aren't trying to put a large amount of food into your freezer in one day. Being a successful freezer cook doesn't mean putting 100+ entrées into your freezer in a day. It means doing what works for you and your family. Mini-sessions are the way to go for lots of cooks. It could mean cooking every night for a week but making three of each; one to eat that night and two to put into the freezer. It won't take long to build up a nice selection. For some, a mini-session means limiting the recipes to what they can accomplish in 3-4 hours. Wouldn't it be great to get up early one Saturday morning a month and know that by noon you could have an extra 10-15 meals in the freezer? It's also a good idea to start with mini-sessions until you get comfortable with freezer cooking. There's nothing better than success to keep you motivated!

Using the "what's-on-sale" approach to freezer cooking can save you lots of money!

Continued on Page 18

#2 What freezer cooking method do I want to use?

Continued from page 17

Three Ways to Freezer Cook:

3. Cook BIG!

Cooking big can mean anything from 30 entrées in one day to 120 entrées over a weekend to anything in between. When Tara and I started cooking together in 1993, we set out to put 30 entrées in each of our freezers by day's end. At first, that was difficult. It took us awhile to get the process down "pat" and choose the right combination of recipes to accomplish our goal. But once we did the 30-meals-in-a-day process for a year or so, we started getting pretty good at it. It seemed like a month went by really quickly so we decided to try doing two months at a time. We were surprised to find out that it didn't take us twice as long to assemble twice as many entrées. The trick, we realized, was making multiples of recipes. The mixture for 6 meatloaves doesn't take much longer to combine than the mixture for 3. So we cooked every two months for awhile and then decided to go bigger. We began cooking "quarterly" and loved it! Over two days, with a lot of good planning and prep work, we each put about 75-80 entrées (we threw a few sides and desserts in there too) in our freezers. Wow – that was great! It worked really well at that time in our lives. Again, just do whatever works best for you. Don't feel like you have to cook BIG to *really* be a freezer cook. Anytime you do a little planning ahead and put anything in the freezer you're "doing it".

Tips for Cooking Big

- Planning is the key. Extra trips to the store for milk or freezer bags will chew up precious time.
- Do as much prep work ahead of time as possible. You don't want to be standing around watching turkey breasts boil on cooking day. Leave a day or two between the shopping and cooking to do your prep work. This is a lot of work and you will be tired!
- Choose the right combination of recipes. Don't do too many labor and time intensive recipes. Cooking up ground beef and measuring it off into 2-1/2 C. portions counts as a recipe!
- Put your recipes in order ahead of time. Starting your first slow cooker meal at 5 p.m. or putting the chicken in marinade for 5 hours at the end of the day is not a good thing. (Don't ask how I know this.)
- Label your foods before putting them into the freezer. Once entrées are flattened in a freezer bag and frozen, they tend to all look the same. When you cook BIG, it's hard to remember what you put into the freezer. (We call this "brain freeze".)

Cooking BIG means a long day and lots of groceries but it's well worth it!

Step #1
Plan It!

Set Dates for Planning, Shopping and Cooking.

Whether you are cooking solo or with a friend, you need a little time to plan. The first time you plan, it will seem to take forever. Going through recipes, thinking of what your family likes, and discussing it all is very time consuming. But you WILL get much quicker!

Put your planning time on your calendar and don't let anything keep you from it! At this time, you also need to set your dates for shopping and cooking. Consult your calendar and leave yourself plenty of time to get the work done. I have heard from a few cooks who tried to plan, shop, and cook in a 24 hour time period. Not a good idea. Planning the day the store ads come out, shopping a few days later and cooking the next day seems to work well.

Fill out the On-Hand Inventory List
(Worksheet A)
Update this list each month before your planning time and have it with you when you sit down to decide on your recipes and tally your ingredients.

If you cook with a friend or a group, you may decide to keep certain items in stock that are only used for your freezer cooking ventures. You might stock rice, tomato paste, pasta, cheeses (frozen), freezer bags, canned tomatoes, frozen diced onions, cooking oil, spices, flour, salt, oatmeal, and other items that you find that you use consistently. Many of these items can be bought ahead on super sales and stored for later use. Be sure to keep track of these on your Inventory List.

When taking inventory, actually *look* inside your spice cans and canisters to determine how much you have. Many a freezer cook has made the mistake of assuming that there was plenty and ended up short on Cooking Day!

Whether you are cooking alone or with others, take the "Pantry Challenge". You will save money and space if you use up what you have first rather than re-buying things you already have. "Guesstimate" the value of these items so that each cook pays her fair share. One *Worksheet A* for each cook's inventory is best, but after each cook has filled one out, it helps to start a new list for the combined totals of each ingredient.

It may seem trivial to the uninitiated to have to actually write down where the different inventory items are stored, but if pantry space is limited, you may actually have a case of tomatoes in your linen closet, garage or basement. Tara and I lost a case of mushrooms once, only to stumble upon it months later with the expiration dates long past. Lost and wasted food won't save you any money!

Make sure to take inventory of non-food items that you will need too. Freezer bags, rigid containers, trash bags, dish soap, and disinfectants are all things you may find that you need to purchase for Cooking Day.

Worksheet A Sample

ITEM NAME	QUANTITY	STORAGE PLACE	VALUE
Quick brown rice	3 lbs.	Pantry	$1.50
Whole peeled tomatoes	3/12 oz. cans	Pantry	$2.50
Elbow macaroni	8 lbs.	Pantry	$5.50
Shredded cheddar cheese	5 lbs.	Freezer	$15.00
Canned sliced mushrooms	4/10 oz. cans	Pantry	$3.00
Milk	2 gallons	Refrigerator	$4.50
Eggs	2 dozen	Refrigerator	$1.50
Mayonnaise	32 oz.	Pantry	$2.00

Step #1

Plan It!

Choose your recipes.

■ Try recipes out first.

Never make more than one of something until you know that it's a "winner". That includes the 30 Day Gourmet recipes in this book and on our website. Yes, I love them and so do most of our cooks but I wouldn't want you to make 6 recipes of *Parsley Parmesan Chicken* unless you're sure that you love it too.

■ Decide how many entrées you want to make.

We freezer cooks get a bad rap sometimes because once we begin this venture people expect us to eat an "out-of-the-freezer home-cooked meal" every night. But most of us don't live that way. I know I don't. Be realistic. Freezer cooking is about doing what works for YOU. If you still want to eat out on Sundays and order pizza on Friday nights, that's fine. Plan for it. You're down to 5 dinners a week now. Is there a night when you always clean up the leftovers? Plan for it. Do you eat at Mom's every Monday night? No reason to stop now.

■ Decide how often you want to freezer cook.

If you're planning to be a once-a-month cook who needs about 20-25 entrées, we suggest that you choose about 6-8 recipes and make 3 of each. If you cook more often than that, you should still do several recipes but you will be building up a variety over more than one cooking day.

■ Make multiples.

Once you're sure of a recipe, always make more than one. Even if you are doing a "mini-session", make multiples. You can put 15-20 chicken entrées into the freezer on a Saturday morning if you choose 3-4 recipes and make 5 of each. The time you save really adds up. All of our recipes are multiplied out in columns making it very easy to make multiples. We've done the hard math problems for you.

■ Don't choose too many or too few recipes.

I realize that you need variety, but don't be like the cook we met once who loved eating the foods but hated the process. She worked all day, all night and half of the next day to get 30 entrées into the freezer. Upon closer questioning, we learned that she was making 30 *different* entrées. Whew – no wonder she hated it. Your family will eat something more than once a month. If they won't, you need to get a new family. But don't be like the ladies who confessed that they only assembled 4 recipes but made 7 of each and began rotating them every night for a month. Lasagna seven times a month?! Probably not. It only took them one cooking day to take a closer look at their recipe list.

■ Choose a few versatile recipes.

Rotating 6 recipes may not seem like much variety to you. Try choosing a few recipes that can be frozen in one form but transformed into different entrées on serving day. For example, I always make hundreds of meatballs. I pre-cook them and freeze them in family-sized portions. On the day that I want to serve them, they could quickly become *Spaghetti and Meatballs*, *Sweet and Sour Meatballs* or *Swedish Meatballs*. Sometimes I made the sauces ahead of time, sometimes not. The meatballs are the hard part and they're done.

■ Always do a slow cooker meal.

Slow cookers are great. You're not limited to using them for wintertime soups and stews. Sandwich fillings, macaroni and cheese and all sorts of other foods can be done in the slow cooker. You can start a recipe the night before cooking day and when you wake up you already have one meal done.

Step #1 Plan It!

Choose Your Recipes.

Be sure that your recipe can be frozen.

■ Food in your freezer, as long as it is at 0 degrees F. or below, does not spoil or become harmful to you. More foods freeze well than not. All of the recipes in this manual and on our website freeze fine. It would be impossible for me to cover every particular food or food ingredient here. The internet provides a wealth of information about freezing at your fingertips. If you have a question about a particular food that I haven't covered, do a quick search and an answer is bound to pop up in a moment. You can also check the information that came with your freezer (you do keep that stuff, right?)

When incorporating your own recipes into the system, be sure to use the following guidelines:

■ Don't thaw frozen raw meat and then re-freeze it without cooking it thoroughly first. For example, many of us purchase ground beef when we see it on sale. We keep it frozen until our next cooking day. That beef will need to be thawed and cooked before it can be re-frozen so we use it in recipes like *Cheeseburger Quiche, Zippy Spaghetti Sauce* or *Taco Chili.* If we want to make meatloaf but not pre-cook it before we freeze it, we will plan to use fresh ground beef. Frozen poultry can be thawed, simmered or baked and used for recipes like *Country Chicken Pot Pie, Chicken Divan,* or *Chicken Hot Pockets.*

■ Hard-boiled eggs tend to get rubbery after thawing. If you chop them up in very fine pieces they are okay.

■ Cornstarch-thickened sauces, cheese sauces and gravies made with milk tend to separate when being reheated after freezing. These sauces are fine when they are mixed with other ingredients like the *White Sauce* recipe I use for our *Chicken Divan.*

■ Don't freeze raw vegetables unless they have been blanched. Blanching is a short period of cooking that seals in color, texture, vitamins and

flavor. (See chart on page 133) Purchased frozen vegetables have already been blanched and can be used "as is". Using these can save you LOTS of prep time. I always use frozen potatoes, broccoli, beans and corn. It's best to stir these into your recipe after it has cooled and is ready to go into the freezer. The quality will be better if the veggies don't thaw and then re-freeze.

■ Exceptions to the veggie blanching rule are diced onions, green pepper and celery. Chop and use!

■ Cured meats, like ham or bacon, should be eaten within a month of freezing. They will lose color and flavor after that.

■ Be aware that some seasonings change in intensity and flavor. Salt loses some of its flavor in freezing and may cause an off-flavor in high fat items. You can salt after thawing if you wish. Celery and green pepper also lose a little flavor. Black pepper, cloves, bay leaves, onions, sage, and artificial vanilla become stronger in flavor.

■ Deep fried foods will not stay crispy after thawing and re-heating. The high fat content may also alter the flavor with time.

■ Egg and milk substitutes freeze well in most recipes.

■ Fully cooked pasta, dry beans and rice tend to turn mushy when frozen in liquids or sauces. Undercook them by half the recommended time if you plan to stir them into a sauce or broth before freezing.

■ Salad vegetables like lettuce, cucumbers, tomatoes and radishes don't freeze well. Actually they freeze fine – it's the thawing and eating that is a problem!

Thaw and cook previously frozen meat to use in your recipes.

Step #1 Plan It!

Reading the Recipes.

One of the unique features of the 30 Day Gourmet system is in the formatting of our recipes. We learned early on that multiplying endless ingredients on cooking day wasn't a good idea. 1/3 x 5? 4 1/2 x 3? These are not easy math problems to do while assembling 30 entrées. Lots of mistakes are made using the "math in your head" method and you end up doing the same process over and over each time you cook. There's a better way. All of the recipes in this manual as well as the ones on our website and in our eBooks are already multiplied out in 6 columns. This makes it easy for you to try out a recipe (follow the "1" column), double a recipe ("2" column) or to cook with a friend and make 6 of a recipe so that you can each take home 3.

Each of our recipes has some consistent features.

- **Title**: Our recipes all fall into 8 categories. This makes it easy for cooks who put their recipes into a binder (FYI – we sell one with tabbed dividers on our website) to keep them organized. Beef – Poultry – Pork & Fish – Meatless – Breads & Breakfast – Soups & Sandwiches – Sides & Salads – Snacks & Desserts
- **Recipes**: Our columns are arranged by the number of recipes not servings. The "1" column is one recipe, the "6" column is 6 recipes.
- **Servings:** To help you plan and because of the nutritional information given, we tell you how many servings there are in each recipe. For example our *Cheeseburger Quiche* recipe yields 6 servings per recipe.
- **Makes:** For some recipes, we tell you how much each recipe makes or yields. This information is useful when you stir up ingredients in one big bowl and then need to portion them down to separate entrées. If a recipe doesn't include this information, you can usually figure it out by using a large measuring cup when combining ingredients and then doing some simple division.

- **Ingredients**: Our ingredients are listed down the left side of each recipe. We have given you the ingredient in the form that it goes into the recipe. For example, in the *Cheeseburger Quiche* recipe we list Ground Beef, cooked rather than Ground Beef, uncooked. It's much easier to tally up your ingredients this way.
- **Assembly Directions**: Each recipe gives you directions for assembling the recipe. Whenever possible, assemble as many recipes as you can in one large mixing container. If the recipe doesn't indicate how many cups per recipe, make a note of that for dividing things up evenly later.
- **Freezing and Cooking Directions**: Some recipes need to be pre-cooked before freezing but many can just be assembled, frozen and then cooked on the day that you want to eat it. In many cases, we give you directions for both options. Most of the cooking directions given in our recipes assume that you have thawed the recipe ahead of time. If you are like me and prefer to decide what's for dinner about 5 p.m. that's okay too. Cooking your entrées from the frozen state is fine. Just increase the cook time by half. In other words, the lasagna that takes 1 hour from the thawed state will take 1 1/2 hours from the frozen state.
- **Comments**: This is where we try to help you out with possible ingredient substitutions, time or money-savers or tips and tricks.
- **Nutritional Information**: These are per serving and are based on the ingredients in the printed list.

Formatting your own Recipes.

To make the 30 Day Gourmet system work for everyone, you need to be able to bring your own recipes into the mix. *Worksheet B* on page 39 is a Recipe Worksheet that you can reproduce and use to format your own recipes. For those pesky math problems, look at another recipe or use the multiplication chart in the Appendix. This Worksheet is also available in the Members section of our website. You can fill it out online or print it off and fill it in by hand.

Step #1 ■ Plan It!

Plan your containers.

Freezer bags.

These are my containers of choice but that's just me. When I began freezer cooking, I didn't have much extra space and I found these to be very efficient for stacking in my small chest freezer. I also like the fact that I can put off my dinner decision until late in the day and still be able to thaw my masterpiece quickly.

■ Make sure that you purchase *freezer* bags and not food storage bags. The freezer bags really are designed for the job.

■ Use a permanent marker to label the bags with the contents and date *before* putting food in the bag. Write simple cooking instructions on the bag. It will save you (or someone else if you're lucky) searching for the manual to make dinner.

■ Bags should not be re-used unless they contain only breadcrumbs or other dry ingredients. Washing the bags in hot water doesn't ensure that you have killed all harmful bacteria. Seams and seals can also be weakened by washing. Who wants to take that chance?

■ Don't put hot foods into freezer bags. Wait until they cool down.

■ Foods with sharp bones like pork chops or steaks that might puncture a bag should be double bagged or frozen in rigid containers. Leaking bags make a big mess!

■ A nine or ten inch pie or quiche dish will fit into most 1-gallon freezer bags. A 9x13x2 baking pan without handles will fit into a 2-gallon freezer bag as will many other shapes of baking dishes.

■ Freeze your bags in thin, flat layers. Remove all possible air and then seal the bag. The air can be removed by a couple of methods.

The Squeegee Method:

Seal the bag from one corner to the other, leaving just a small opening at one end. Use the palm of your hand to work the air from the bottom of the bag to the top. Flatten the bag as you go. When all possible air is out, finish sealing the bag. This method works best for soft, formless foods like stew, chicken and noodles and meatloaf mixture.

The Straw Method:

Place cooled food or a pan containing food in a freezer bag. Insert an ordinary drinking straw in one corner of the bag opening. Seal the bag from one corner all the way to the straw in the other corner. Pinch the straw and corner of the bag tightly together to keep air from escaping, then suck out the excess air. When the air is removed, quickly pull out the straw and finish sealing the bag. This method works with lumpy foods like chicken parts, fish fillets, steaks and chops. It also works well for freezing foods right in the serving dish like a casserole or baked quiche. It is very important that you do not touch the straw to raw meats, into marinades or sauces or into crumbs.

Freeze your foods in thin, flat layers for efficient stacking and thawing.

The Vacuum-sealer Method:

Vacuum sealers are great inventions. The lower priced sealers are only useful when you want to remove all possible air and form a vacuum (like a bag of chicken parts). To vacuum seal liquids (like soup or stew) you need to use the sealer that allows you to stop the suction and seal the bag.

Continued on Page 24

Plan Your Containers

Continued from page 23

Rigid plastic freezer containers

These are very common now and can be found at your local grocery store, discount store or home party dealer. Rigid containers are great if you have a freezer with plenty of stacking space where they can be easily organized. Plastic containers can be re-used until they crack or the seal no longer fits tightly. Containers manufactured specifically for the freezer can be expensive but last much longer. Experiment with the different sizes offered. I like to use the individual serving sized containers for lunch items and frozen salads. The goal is to choose the size container that will keep you from thawing, cooking and/or serving and then re-freezing the leftovers.

Do not pour very hot or boiling foods into plastic containers. Cool the foods first and allow adequate space at the top of the container for expansion. About 1/2 inch of air at the top of a quart of liquids is plenty.

Freezer labels should be applied to your containers *before* freezing them. Good-sized labels can be hard to find. For that reason, we sell customized 30 Day Gourmet labels that can be ordered from our website. Our labels are 2"x3" – large enough for a title, date, quantity and directions. These labels become stronger in the freezer and revert to removable adhesive at room temperature. Masking tape works sometimes but often peels off in the freezer. And don't even think of NOT labeling your foods. You do know that everything looks the same once it's frozen don't you?

Glass and ceramic dishes

Combined foods such as casseroles may be frozen in the dishes they will be cooked in and served from. When the food in the dish has cooled, it can be wrapped with freezer-weight foil or freezer paper or slid into a large freezer bag. The advantage of freezing in glass and ceramic is that you can freeze, defrost, bake and refrigerate all in the same container. This is convenient and cost effective. The one disadvantage is that dishes will take up more space in your freezer because they usually aren't uniform sizes. The other

Find the freezer container combination that works best for you.

disadvantage, of course, is in not having enough dishes. Try garage sales, estate auctions and dollar stores. It won't take long to build up a supply.
Caution: Do not put a frozen glass or ceramic dish in a hot oven. You risk shattering your container but even worse losing your dinner! Thaw these foods in the refrigerator or microwave first.

Disposable or re-usable metal or foil pans

The disadvantage of foil pans is that they are generally fairly flimsy and may not stack well until completely and firmly frozen. They are great for one-time use and can come in handy for meals that you plan to freeze and give as a gift. Aluminum pans will also react chemically to highly acidic foods like tomato sauce and vinegar. You may not want to freeze lasagna or Italian casseroles in aluminum – the flavor may be affected and the pan may even be damaged.

Another option if you don't have many metal, glass or ceramic dishes is to use the "frozen block" trick. Line your baking dish with good quality plastic wrap or foil and leave a few inches extra on the edges. Assemble your cooled recipe ingredients on top of the wrap. Place the assembled recipe on a level surface in the freezer and allow it to freeze until firm. Remove the dish from the freezer and set it on the counter. Grasp the wrap with your hands and pop the firm block of food out of the dish. Either finish wrapping the food with more plastic wrap or foil, or place it inside a freezer bag.

There are as many freezer container options as there are foods that will freeze. Experiment a little and find the combination of containers that works best for you.

Step #1 ■ Plan It!

Plan your shopping.

Fill out the Tally Sheet (*Worksheet C*) on pages 40 & 41. Our lay-flat binding allows you to open the manual flat and lay it on a copier. Software savvy cooks may want to check out our 30 Day Gourmet Advantage Cooking Software. It comes pre-loaded with all of the recipes in this manual plus 20 others. The software does all of the tally work for you.

Use the sample tally sheet below as a guide. Finalize your list of recipes and write them in the left hand column of *Worksheet C*. Follow the directions below to fill out the form. Filling out this form will give you a complete list of all ingredients and other essentials you will need on Assembly Day.

WORKSHEET C – TALLY SHEET

Note: These directions are for Worksheet C which can be found on pages 40 and 41.

Directions:

1. Write the name of your first recipe on lines 1 and 1a. Fill in the amount of meals you will make of each recipe.

2. In the diagonal columns, fill in the needed ingredients. Going horizontally across lines 1 and 1a, fill in the correct amounts of each ingredients.

3. Repeat the process for each recipe. Be sure to account for freezer bags, oils, trash bags, etc.

4. Once all of your ingredients have been accounted for, go down the chart vertically and tally the TOTAL AMOUNT NEEDED of each ingredient.

5. Take out your On-Hand Inventory Sheet (*Worksheet A*) and list what you have on hand in the –Total on Hand box. Be sure to add these inventory items to your list of What to Bring on Assembly Day (*Worksheet E*).

6. Do the math (it's simple subtraction) and you should be left with your TOTALS TO BUY.

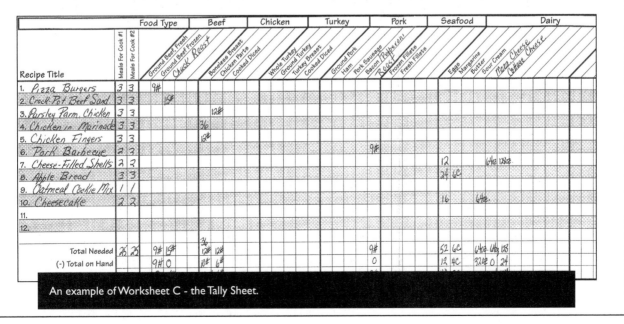

An example of Worksheet C - the Tally Sheet.

Step #1 ■ Plan It!

Plan your shopping.

Fill out the Shopping List (*Worksheet D*) on page 42. Transfer the ingredients and numbers from the "Total Needed" line on the Tally Sheet (*Worksheet C*) to the appropriate columns on your Shopping List (*Worksheet D*).

■ Check your grocery advertisements and decide where to get what. It really pays to shop around, especially when buying large quantities. In our area, at least one of the chain stores is usually running chicken and beef on sale. Some stores have a price-matching policy which could save you time also.

Worksheet D Sample

Beef	Canned foods	Frozen Foods	Oils
Fresh ground, 7 lbs.	Tomato sauce, 132 oz.	Broccoli cuts, 2 lbs.	Canola oil, 12 oz.
Stew beef, 6 lbs.	Tomato paste, 8 oz.	Carrots, 1 lb.	Olive oil 6 oz.
Chuck roast, 5 lbs.	Kidney beans, 2 lbs.	Peas, 20 oz.	
	Crushed garlic, 3 oz.	Sliced mushrooms, 10 oz.	
		Diced onions, 3 lbs.	
Chicken	**Grains**	**Fresh Produce**	**Mixes**
Fresh parts, 8 lbs.	Quick brown rice, 16 oz.	Broccoli, 4 lg. bunches	Taco seas pkts., 4
Boneless breast, 4 lbs.	Wild rice, 8 oz.	Green onions, 2 bunches	Onion soup mix, 2
Thighs, 6 lbs.		Red sweet peppers, 3	
		Green peppers, 2	
Turkey	**Pasta**	**Spices**	**Staples**
Frozen breasts, 12 lbs.	Elbow macaroni, 12 oz.	Oregano, 1.5 oz.	Flour, 5 lbs.
	Spaghetti, 16 oz.	Thyme, 1 oz.	Red wine vinegar, 8 oz.

■ You may use a different shopping list for each store you will visit, or use one list and highlight each store's specials with a different color. If you are splitting the shopping chores with a cooking partner, be very careful not to overlap ingredients on your lists, or you will buy more than you need!

Tips to Plan Your Shopping:

■ Write in the total pounds, ounces, cups, etc. of each item. For example, canned whole tomatoes are sold by the ounce. Rather than writing "*6/28 ounce cans*", write "*whole canned tomatoes/168 oz.*" By doing this, you might see that you can buy one food service size can, meaning less time with the can opener. Take a hand-held calculator with you when you shop for making on-the-spot conversions.

■ Use the Equivalency Charts on pages 128-131 to assist you in figuring totals.

■ In the miscellaneous column, include such things as freezer bags, foil, freezer labels, rubber gloves, trash bags, permanent markers, dish soap, and snacks and lunch for Assembly Day.

■ When you know what quantities you need, call the supermarket meat counter in advance and ask about quantity discounts, limits, and bulk packaging.

■ The meat department will also grind special meats for you, mix different ground meats together thoroughly, slice large cuts, cube steaks and do many other helpful things. Just ask early enough to give them adequate time to fill your order.

■ You can buy jars of chopped, minced, or pureed garlic in the produce section of your grocery store. This will save you a lot of "clove crushing".

■ Buy frozen diced onions in the frozen vegetable case in the supermarket. This will spare you a lot of tears!

Step #1 — Plan It!

Plan your prep work

Use the sample page below to help you decide what you want to try to accomplish before the Big Day arrives. If you are cooking with a partner, it helps to divide up the chores ahead of time.

Writing down what each cook needs to bring is so helpful. Otherwise, the traveling cook will be standing in her kitchen trying to remember that last item that she said she would bring. Of course, she won't remember until 4 hours later when she is knee-deep in meatball mixture and remembers that she forgot her cookie scoop!

Worksheet E Sample

What To Do Before Assembly Day	
Cook # 1	**Cook # 2**
Brown ground beef - 5 lbs.	Make 24 cups of white sauce
Dice all celery	Cook 2 lbs. pasta
Dice 3 lbs. of ham	Skin all chicken parts
Grind 2 lbs. of ham	Shred 1 lb. Swiss cheese
Cook all dry beans	Shred 1 lb. carrots
Steam all diced onions and celery	Cook 24 oz. brown rice
Start one slow cooker meal the night before	Start one slow cooker meal the night before

What To Bring On Assembly Day	
Cook # 1	**Cook # 2**
Large cookware	Large measuring cups
Long handled utensils	Cutting boards
Inventory and prep work foods	Inventory and prep work foods
Freezer bags	Freezer bags
Foil	Food processor
Slow cooker	Slow cooker
Cookie scoop	Coolers and cardboard boxes

All kinds of work can be done ahead of time - making the kids do it is even smarter!

Make it easier with a little planning....

Step #2
Shop! Shop! Shop!

Before you go. . .

- Clean out your refrigerator and freezer. You will need as much room as possible for the many groceries you will be bringing home. You should not leave perishable ingredients at room temperature for more than two hours.

- Be sure you allow yourself enough time to get the job done. It's much easier to do it all at once than to go out 4 different times.

When to go. . .

- Although you can stock up on non-perishable items all month long as you watch for sales, the perishable groceries and meats that you want to start with fresh should be purchased no more than 2 or 3 days before Assembly Day.

- Be sure to leave yourself enough time to get your prep work done. If you make the mistake (like I have) of not shopping until the evening before Assembly Day, then you end up being on your feet for what seems like 3 days straight!

- People may get a little impatient waiting for you to check out at the supermarket if you have massive amounts and it is at a peak sales time. Be extra considerate and shop during the "off" hours. Try shopping during early morning, early afternoon, or late evening - anything to avoid the "rush hours".

What to take. . .

Wear comfortable clothing and take the following:
- Tally Sheet (*Worksheet C*)
- Shopping List (*Worksheet D*)
- Prep Work List (*Worksheet E*)
- Coolers during warm weather
- Adequate cash, checks or credit cards
- Calculator
- Store advertisements
- Extra bags and boxes
- Sense of humor

More Shopping Day Tips:

- Buying your food items in large quantities may save you some money and the time it takes opening, using, and throwing away many small cans or jars. We look for items like Worcestershire sauce, vinegar, soy sauce, and cooking oil in 1-gallon containers.

- If you are cooking with a partner, organize your groceries as you put them on the belt and separate them by "what goes where". Each cook has her own "to do" list before Assembly Day (*Worksheet E*). Having each cook's ingredients in separated bags or boxes is very helpful.

- Grocers will sometimes waive the limits on advertised specials if you order large quantities and call 3-4 days in advance of when you need to pick them up.

- Try to put refrigerated and frozen items in your cart last, so they stay cold longer.

- Be sure to check expiration dates. Don't purchase dented canned goods.

Planning ahead is the key to saving time and money on Assembly Day.

Do your prep work

Try to think of this project as a "cooking week". Of course, it doesn't take a whole week, but there are things that HAVE to be done ahead if this is going to work. Just remember, if you have chosen 8-10 recipes and make 3 of each, you will only be doing this once every 4 to 6 weeks and *IT WILL BE WORTH IT!* Think of cooking week in 4 processes - 1. Planning; 2. Shopping; 3. Prep Work; 4. Assembly Day. We've already covered the first 2 processes, so you are half way done!

The rule for Prep Work is:

The more you get done before Assembly Day, the better! Divide these pre-Assembly Day chores among all of the cooks. If you are cooking solo, enlist some help from the family.

- Skin chicken parts
- Cook and drain pasta
- Make coatings for chicken parts
- Start slow cooker meals
- Chop and steam vegetables
- Brown ground meats
- Dice or grind ham
- Make sauces
- Cook and dice poultry
- Soak and cook dry beans

As you go, try to separate the items for each recipe into its own bag. For example, all the boneless skinless chicken breasts for the chicken fingers go into one bag, and all the boneless skinless chicken breasts for marinades go into another bag. This will keep you from using up too much chicken breast in the first recipe and not having enough for the next one.

To be honest, there will be some Assembly Days when you will start with very few of these things done. It will make for a much longer Assembly Day, but it was better than not cooking at all. Don't be too hard on yourself.

It also helps to explain what you are about to embark on to your family and friends. They need to know that this will require a big time commitment from you, but that the results will be worth it. Go over your cooking week schedule with them and ask them to help you with tasks like carrying in groceries, caring for small children, and helping with simple meal preparations while you do other important tasks to get ready for Assembly Day (it is okay to send them out to eat).

If you are traveling to a cooking partner's house:

- Put as much "stuff" in your vehicle the night before as possible.
- Post your copy of *Worksheet E* in a prominent place and check it frequently.
- Turn your freezer to its coldest temperature in readiness for the foods you will bring home.
- Arrange your freezer to accommodate the new foods.

If you are hosting the Assembly Day:

- Remove all unneeded items from your kitchen counters and work spaces.
- Empty your trash and have a large empty trash container for each cook on hand.
- Set out your mixing bowls, pans, utensils, etc.
- Turn your freezer to its coldest temperature.
- Arrange your freezer to accommodate the new foods you will put into it.
- Line all work spaces with several layers of clean newsprint. This is a big help with clean-up tasks. As you drip or spill on it, just roll up that layer and discard it.

Clean out your refrigerator (and freezer) BEFORE you go shopping!

Step #4 ■
Now We're Cooking!

Items needed for each cook:

Long handled utensils:
Forks
Slotted spoons
Ladles
Wire whisks
Tongs
Metal/Rubber spatulas

Large containers for mixing:
Dish pans with flat bottoms
Mixing bowls
Water bath canners

Cookware and bakeware:
Two large rimmed baking sheets
Two 9"x13"x2" baking pans
One or two 2-quart glass dishes
One paring knife
One chopping knife
One slicing knife
Two sets of standard measuring cups
Two sets of standard measuring spoons
One deep, covered pan or one stock pot
One cutting board
One large 12" skillet with a lid
One 2-quart covered saucepan
One colander (large strainer)
Two oven mitts
Two pot holders
One kitchen timer
One 2-cup glass measure

Items that are great to have:
Microwaveable containers
Mixing bowls with handles and spouts
Extra kitchen timers
Electric hand mixer
Large, lidded containers for marinating
Electric stand mixer
Large-sized sets of measuring cups
Electric can opener
Electric skillets/hot plates
Food processor or blender
Spring mechanism cookie scoops
Slow cooker
Large electric roasting pans
Large pastry brush
4-cup glass measure
Bulb baster

Each cook needs her/his own set of basic items but only use as many dishes as you are willing *to wash!*

"Can't cook without-'em" Assembly Day basics for Nanci

Step #4 ■
Now We're Cookin'!

Assembly Day Procedures

Cooks attempting to assemble 30 entrées should plan on an 8-10 hour day although I've heard from several people using our system who work much faster. On the IDEAL Assembly Day, you will have no kids to watch, no lunch to fix, and nowhere to be that night. Your husband will take the kids out to dinner and then bring them home and put them to bed. Then he will rub your feet and say, "*Honey, why don't you go soak in the tub while I finish cleaning up.*" On REAL Assembly Days, you may have a sick child, nothing for lunch, and three evening meetings you are expected to attend. I just don't want you to get frustrated striving for perfection. No one has the perfect cooking partner, mate, kids, or schedule. Be flexible. You'll live longer!

■ **Post your Tally Sheet (Worksheet C) in a prominent place.**
A kitchen desktop or hanging clip is ideal. You will refer to it throughout the day. It's the only place where you have written down the recipe titles and how many you intend to assemble of each.

■ **Organize your recipes.**
Take a few minutes to organize your recipes. Group them by type. Chicken, Beef, Side Dishes, etc. Then sort them by which one needs to be started first. If you are making *Parsley Parmesan Chicken,* the recipe calls for soaking the parts in Italian dressing for at least 4 hours. Best to do that first! Then get that crock pot recipe started. I like to start with a few "quick" recipes. It gives you an early feeling of accomplishment and some extra storage space in your refrigerator.

■ **Finish your prep work.**
If you didn't finish all of your prep work (or do anything ahead of time), get out *Worksheet E* and see if there are things that you should do now. If the white sauce that you will use in 3 recipes, hasn't been made you'll want to do that now rather than in the middle of the first recipe that calls for it. Same with chopping veggies or boiling and dicing poultry or browning ground beef. Get it done first thing.

■ **Begin assembling entrées.**
Our method is simple. Work one type at a time, one recipe at a time. Start with the chicken, then do the beef, then do the rest. If you are cooking with a partner, one cook does the chicken, the other does the beef, and then share the remaining recipes. The chance of cross-contamination from meats is greatly reduced this way because you are not switching back and forth between raw meats. Take your first recipe and check the Tally Sheet (*Worksheet C*) to see how many of that recipe needs to be made. Follow the appropriate column on the recipe and begins assembling the ingredients. If you are cooking with a partner, assemble enough of the recipe for your own *AND* the other cook's entrées. Time is saved by stirring it all up at once! You can also save clean-up time by doing as many recipes using the cooked protein as possible and then moving on to the raw protein. You will just need a quick wipe between recipes that way rather than the full scrub down needed if you switch between cooked and raw. Obviously, there may be times when you will start a new recipe before finishing the last one. If you are waiting for something to bake, don't use that time to watch a 30-minute television show because the rules say "one recipe at a time". The point is – don't have all 10 recipes going at once. You'll drive yourself nuts. Don't ask how I know this.

■ **Cool and package the recipe.**
Attempt to get your entrées assembled, cooled, packaged, and frozen *as quickly as possible*. Besides the sense of accomplishment, the quality of the food is better because you have gotten it into the freezer as *quickly as possible*.

Step #4 ■
Now We're Cookin'!

Assembly Day Tips

- Get plenty of sleep the night before Assembly Day.
- Assemble and freeze soupy casseroles early in the day so you have a level surface to place them on.
- Start time consuming, slow cooking, or marinating foods early.
- Remember to assemble in large quantities. For example, do not assemble each quiche individually. Combine the ingredients for all of the quiche at the same time and distribute the ingredients equally. This will save lots of time!
- Think about which days are your busiest and pre-cook a few items for those days. They will only need a quick warm-up.
- Line baking sheets with foil between each batch of a recipe like broiled meatballs for easier clean up. This frees up the pan for the next batch.
- Use as few pots, pans, and utensils as possible and wash well between recipes. This makes clean up easier and forces you to wash your hands several times that day.
- Leave perishable ingredients in the refrigerator until they are needed. This can be difficult when making large quantities. In the winter, you may be able to use your porch or garage. Coolers with ice packs might do the trick. Look at what's taking up the most space and try to use up those items first.
- Choose your freezer container sizes wisely. Portion your recipes down into what will be eaten at one time. This will cut down on leftovers and food waste.
- Just a word of encouragement - the day will be half over before it seems like you get anything done!
- Wear good supportive shoes and exchange them with another pair halfway through the day.
- Tall kitchen stools allow you to sit and work at the same time.
- Play upbeat music to help you keep a good pace.
- Take a lunch break and put your feet up.
- Use a LARGE trashcan! If you are cooking with a partner, use two. None of this cute-little-trashcan-under- the-sink stuff.
- If you are cooking with a partner, keep your conversations positive and uplifting. Gossip is destructive and your friend will tire of it quickly.
- Be clean! Please shower, wash your hair, and pull it back. Brush your teeth!
- Let your answering machine or voice mail do its job. Answering the phone chews up too much time!
- Hire a babysitter for the children, or better yet, trade childcare with another 30 Day Gourmet!
- If children must be on the premises, keep them happy! Check out some new books and videos. Set up a self-serve snack table.
- Keep your beverages in sport drink cups that have lids, handles, and extra long straws. Food cannot fall into them, and the drink will not spill out if you knock it over. The handle keeps your hands away from your germs, and the food bacteria away from you!
- Wear an apron. Having a couple of pockets for your marking pen and labels is very handy.
- Cover all of your work surfaces with several sheets of clean newsprint to catch spills and drips.
- Enjoy a couple of snacks throughout the day to keep your energy level up.
- Remember to stop and admire your work occasionally. You are accomplishing great things!

A cookie scoop make quick work of meatballs. The foil cuts down on clean-up time.

Step #5 ■
Stocking the Freezer

Freezing Info

■ Remember to fill out your Meal Inventory Checklist *(Worksheet F)* as you put your foods into the freezer. Don't think that you will fill it out later. Sometimes what's on the Tally Sheet doesn't exactly match what you actually have because you might portion one recipe down into 3 containers.

■ Use bags and containers designed for the freezer. They really do work much better. Save your whipped topping containers for draining car oil. If the bag or container isn't labeled as being suitable for freezer use, then it probably isn't.

■ Label bags and containers *before* filling them. Some markers won't work on warm or cold surfaces. Many freezer labels won't stick to cold containers.

■ Label all foods clearly. Many foods look the same when frozen. When cooking with a partner, initial each container of food or designate separate shelves so they are easy to divide later.

■ Packaging foods in thin, flat freezer bags or in small, flatter rigid containers will help them freeze faster and will help to protect the flavor, color, moisture content and nutritional value of your foods.

■ Keep your freezer temperature at 0 degrees F or colder and keep the door shut as much as possible to maintain top quality. Do not attempt to save energy by raising the temperature of frozen food storage above 0 degrees F.

■ Temperatures that fluctuate up and down cause the ice in foods to thaw slightly and then refreeze. Each time this happens, small ice crystals become larger and you lose quality. The food is still safe to eat, it may just lose some texture and/or taste.

■ If your family opens your freezer often for ice cream, popsicles, or convenience foods, consider storing those foods in your refrigerator's freezer and saving your extra freezer for your 30 Day Gourmet foods. The opposite plan will work too.

■ Don't try to freeze hot or warm foods. It will make your freezer work less efficiently and cause ice crystals to form all over your food. Cool foods before packaging them.

■ Spread your freezer foods out as much as possible so that the air can circulate freely. This will freeze the foods more quickly. Once the food is frozen, packages can be restacked closer together.

■ If you have trouble getting your food to freeze quickly, you may be trying to put too much in at one time. Do not freeze more than 3 lbs. of fresh food per cubic foot of freezer space. In other words, do not freeze more than 30 pounds of new foods in a 10 cu. ft. freezer, or 45 pounds in a 15 cu. ft. freezer. A maximum of 60 pounds of freshly prepared foods should go into a 20 cu. ft. freezer. If you want to freeze more than is recommended, leave some of your foods in the refrigerator overnight and add them when the other food is frozen.

■ If you have a chest freezer, don't put all of one kind of food in a layer. Stagger the foods so that you don't have to dig to the bottom to find what you want. If you do not distribute the foods well, you may get to the bottom of the freezer and discover that you are stuck eating the same recipe 3 times at the end of a month!

■ If you are the visiting cook, consider leaving at least part of your food in the host's freezer (if there is room) until it is frozen solid.

Label all foods before putting them into the freezer. You'll be glad you did!

Step #5
Stocking the Freezer

Freezing Q & A's

What foods can I freeze?

Almost all foods can be frozen. Some, though, won't taste as well after they have been defrosted. Foods that you should never try to freeze are: food in cans, eggs in shells, lettuce, tomatoes, potatoes, radishes, cucumbers, green onion (See page 21 for more specific information). Foods that freeze fine mixed into a recipe, but not alone are: sour cream, mayonnaise, cream cheese and cottage cheese.

Is frozen food safe?

Food stored constantly at 0 degrees F will always be safe. Only the quality suffers with lengthy freezer storage. Freezing preserves food for extended periods because it prevents the growth of microorganisms that cause both food spoilage and foodborne illness.

Can frozen food taste as "fresh" as food cooked without freezing?

Yes, definitely. Freshness and quality at the time of freezing can affect the taste after defrosting. Freeze foods at their peak quality. Freezing foods at 0 degrees F or lower retains vitamin content, color, flavor and texture. More than anything, proper packaging affects the long term quality of frozen foods.

What's the safest and easiest way to defrost foods?

The three safe ways to defrost foods are: in the refrigerator, in cold water or in the microwave. Don't thaw foods on the kitchen counter or outdoors. These methods can leave your foods unsafe to eat.

What is freezer burn and how can I avoid it?

Freezer burn appears as grayish-brown leathery spots on your foods and is caused by air reaching the surface of the food. It doesn't make your food unsafe to eat. Cut freezer-burned portions away. Heavily freezer-burned foods should be discarded for quality reasons.

If my meat changes color in the freezer, it is "bad"?

Color changes occur in frozen foods. The bright red color of meat as purchased usually turns dark or pale brown depending on its variety. Freezing doesn't usually cause color changes in poultry although the bones and the meat near them can become dark. The dulling of color in frozen vegetables and cooked foods is usually the result of excessive drying due to improper packaging or lengthy storage. None of these color changes means that the food is "bad". Food doesn't become unsafe in the freezer.

Is it okay to freeze meats in their grocery store wrapping?

Yes, but this type of wrap is permeable to air. If you won't be using the meat within a month, it's best to overwrap or re-package the meat using heavy duty foil, rigid freezer containers or freezer bags. It isn't necessary to rinse meat and poultry before freezing. Freeze unopened vacuum packages "as is".

What is flash freezing?

Flash freezing or open freezing is when you need to get the food "firmed up" before you package it for long term storage. It usually involves fragile foods that might crush or casseroles that you want to freeze and then "pop out" of their pan and transfer to freezer bags. When you flash freeze or open freeze you can just stick the pan, etc. in the freezer without covering the food. Once it's firm then you pull it out and package it.

Can I re-freeze foods once they have thawed?

According to the USDA, if food has been thawed in the refrigerator, it is safe to refreeze it without cooking although there may be a loss of quality due to the moisture lost during defrosting. This rule only applies if the thawed food has constantly been kept cold.

Can I take my meals straight from the freezer to the oven?

Yes, just increase the cooking time by half. Be careful about putting frozen glass dishes into a hot oven!

Step #5
Stocking the Freezer

Fill out the Meal Inventory Checklist

(Worksheet F) as you put your labeled entrées into the freezer. If you make more than 18 recipes, use two inventory checklists. As you prepare your entrées for the freezer, fill in one of these checklists for each cook (sometimes you end up with more than you planned). Each cook should take the checklist home and put it on the freezer door (or some equally conspicuous place).

Directions:

Place a slash mark in one box for each entree` as it goes into the freezer (this way you can always know how many total entrées you have.) Fill in any ingredients that you will need to purchase or have on hand to serve with each entrée. You may also make a note of an entrée you need to save for a special occasion. As you remove an entrée from the freezer to serve it, cross it off the list.

Worksheet F Sample

<table>
<tr><td colspan="9" align="center">MEAL INVENTORY CHECKLIST

Date_____</td></tr>
<tr><td colspan="6"># Of Recipes Stored</td><td>Recipe</td><td colspan="2">Needed on hand for serving</td></tr>
<tr><td>/</td><td>/</td><td>X</td><td></td><td></td><td></td><td>Taco Chili</td><td colspan="2">Shredded cheese, sour cream, rolls or bread</td></tr>
<tr><td>/</td><td>X</td><td>X</td><td></td><td></td><td></td><td>Crock Pot Beef Sandwiches</td><td colspan="2">Sandwich buns, condiments</td></tr>
<tr><td>/</td><td>X</td><td>X</td><td></td><td></td><td></td><td>Parsley Parmesan Chicken</td><td colspan="2"></td></tr>
<tr><td>/</td><td>/</td><td></td><td></td><td></td><td></td><td>Chicken Fingers</td><td colspan="2">Dips</td></tr>
<tr><td>/</td><td>/</td><td>X</td><td></td><td></td><td></td><td>Ham and Potato Casserole</td><td colspan="2">Cornflake topping, butter</td></tr>
<tr><td>/</td><td>X</td><td></td><td></td><td></td><td></td><td>Turkey Divan</td><td colspan="2">Frozen in components to be assembled after thawing.</td></tr>
<tr><td>X</td><td>X</td><td></td><td></td><td></td><td></td><td>Pork BBQ</td><td colspan="2">Sandwich buns   <u>Serve at picnic on 5th</u></td></tr>
<tr><td>/</td><td>X</td><td></td><td></td><td></td><td></td><td>Cheese-Filled Shells</td><td colspan="2">Spaghetti or marinara sauce, grated parmesan cheese</td></tr>
</table>

Step #5 ■
Stocking the Freezer

Now What?

Clean Up and Evaluate

Leaving yourself some time for cleanup is a good idea. It may take longer than you think, especially if you have not lined your work surfaces with newsprint or limited yourself on the amount of cookware you used. You will be glad if you were diligent in washing your dishes between recipes! At this point, your feet will probably be aching and you'll be a bit slap-happy, but knowing that you have so much food prepared and stashed in your freezer will feel great! Don't be surprised if you do not want to eat them for a few days and keep opening up your freezer door just to marvel and smile!

Try to do a quick evaluation of what went right and wrong. How did it go? What will you do differently next time? Writing your observations on paper will really help you for your next Assembly Day. Be sure to write changes you would like to make on the recipes also. Save your worksheets from each of your

section of this book for helpful information on food safety, safe thawing practices, and much, much more.

Worksheet G Sample

This Monthly Menu Planner can be a great help in planning out your daily meals. Use your Meal Inventory Sheet and your family calendar to help you plan. Remember, being a successful 30 Day Gourmet doesn't mean eating out of the freezer every single night. If you always eat out on Friday nights and have dinner with your parents on Sundays, write it in. Fill in the dates and make notes of what you want to serve on the especially busy days. Also make note of company meals and what you plan to serve. Some cooks like to assign a meal category to each day of the week. **Sunday** – crock pot, **Monday** – Beef, **Tuesday** – Chicken, **Wednesday** – Soup & Sandwiches, **Thursday** – Fish or Pork, **Saturday** – leftovers. Thinking ahead a bit will keep you from using up all of your "fast foods" early in the month or spending the last 5 days before your next Assembly Day eating the same two casseroles. Again, do whatever works for you!

Sunday	Monday	Tuesday	Wednesday	Thursday	Friday	Saturday
	Ballet at 4:30 Chicken Fingers Make ahead Mashed Potatoes Jell-O & carrots	**Soccer at 4:30** Taco Chili Salad Peaches	**Choir at 7:00** Beef Sandwiches Buns Oven fries Green beans	**Soccer at 4:00** Turkey & Noodles Carrot salad Fruit slush	Chicken in a Pot Baked Potatoes Broccoli Canned pears	Lasagna Spinach salad Breadsticks Fruit salad
Church 7:00 Parsley Parm Chicken Stir fry veggies Frozen salad Cookies	**Ballet at 4:30** Burgers Home fries Slaw Apple salad	**Soccer at 4:30** Pizza Dinner W/team in town	**Choir at 7:00** Swiss Steak Italian Noodles	**Soccer at 4:00** Tetrazzini Broccoli salad Orange salad	Grilled Chicken Corn Casserole Grilled veggies	**Soccer game** Dinner with Mom & Dad

cooking adventures. You'll be surprised at how handy this information will be later on.

Read through the planning section occasionally to remind yourself of procedures and tips. You may discover some information that you missed the first time through! Be sure to check out the Appendix

Give yourself a hand! You just planned, shopped, prepared, assembled, packaged, labeled and froze a bunch of great foods for your freezer. Whew! Take a deep breath and relax. Tomorrow you will begin to enjoy all the benefits of being a 30 Day Gourmet.

That's it! You're done! Congratulations and welcome to 30 Day Gourmet cooking!

Planning Worksheets

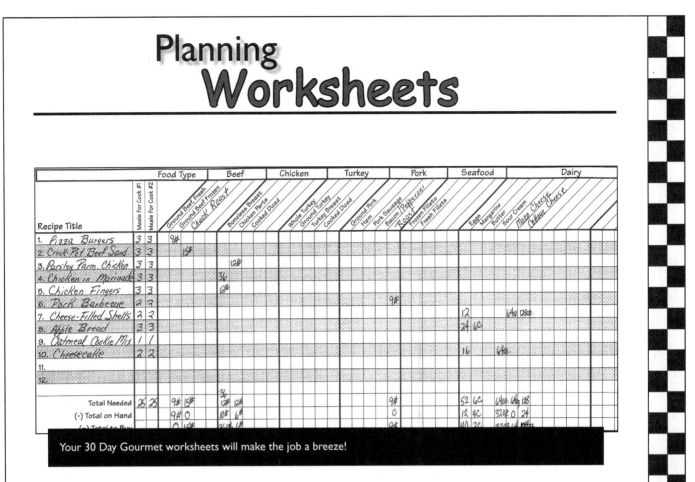

Recipe Title	Meals For Cook #1	Meals For Cook #2	Food Type		Beef			Chicken			Turkey			Pork					Seafood			Dairy				
			Ground Beef Fresh	Ground Beef Frozen / Chuck Roast	Boneless Breast	Chicken Parts	Cooked Diced	Whole Turkey	Ground Turkey	Turkey Breast	Cooked Diced	Ground Pork	Ham	Pork Sausage	Bacon Pepperoni / Roast	Frozen Fillets	Fresh Fillets		Eggs	Margarine	Butter	Sour Cream	Mozz. Cheese	Cottage Cheese			
1. Pizza Burgers	3	3	9#																								
2. Crock-Pot Beef Sand.	3	3		15#																							
3. Parsley Farm Chicken	3	3			12#																						
4. Chicken in Marinade	3	3			36																						
5. Chicken Fingers	3	3			12#																						
6. Pork Barbecue	3	3												9#													
7. Cheese-Filled Shells	2	2																	12				64oz	128oz			
8. Apple Bread	3	3																	24	6c							
9. Oatmeal Cookie Mix	1	1																									
10. Cheesecake	2	2																	16		64oz.						
11.																											
12.																											
Total Needed	26	25	9#	15#	36 / 12# 12#									9#					52	6c	64oz 64oz 128						
(-) Total on Hand			9#	0	10#	8#								0					12	4c	32oz 0 24						
(-) Total to Buy			0	15#	26#	4# 1#								9#					40	2c	32oz						

Your 30 Day Gourmet worksheets will make the job a breeze!

- These worksheets can also be accessed at the Members section of our website. Access info is available on page 3. The Tally Sheet, however, requires 11x17 paper for best use so it's a good idea to take that one to your copy shop.

- This manual uses otabinding, which allows it to lie flat without the pages coming out.

- You will use these worksheets each time you cook so keep this set as a master copy.

- Make 5-10 copies at once. You know how quickly time flies by!

- Please ONLY make copies for yourself. When your friends start begging for your organizational secrets, give them our website address or toll free number. Thanks!

- If you're thinking - there must be a software program that will do all of this "figuring" – you're right! Our 30 Day Gourmet Advantage Software has the functionality to replace most of these worksheets. Check it out at www.30daygourmet.com

Planning Worksheets

ON-HAND INVENTORY LIST			
ITEM NAME	QUANTITY	STORAGE PLACE	VALUE

Planning Worksheets

WORKSHEET B
Recipe Worksheet

CATEGORY:_____

Recipes:	1	2	3	4	5	6
Servings/Makes						
Ingredients:						

Assembly Directions:

Freezing Directions:

Serving Directions:

Comments:

Worksheet C - Tally Sheet

Recipe Title	Meals For Cook #1	Meals For Cook #2	Food Type			Beef			Chicken				Turkey		
			Ground Beef, Fresh	Ground Beef Frozen		Boneless Breast	Chicken Parts	Cooked Diced	Whole Turkey	Ground Turkey	Turkey Breast	Cooked Diced	Ground Pork	Ham	
1.															
2.															
3.															
4.															
5.															
6.															
7.															
8.															
9.															
10.															
11.															
12.															
Total Needed															
(-) Total on Hand															
(=) Total to Buy															

Recipe Title	Meals For Cook #1	Meals For Cook #2	Food Type	Grains, Pasta, Dry Beans, Breads, Crumb Crackers											
1.a														
2.a														
3.a														
4.a														
5.a														
6.a														
7.a														
8.a														
9.a														
10.a														
11.a														
12.a														
Total Needed														
(-) Total on Hand														
(=) Total to Buy														

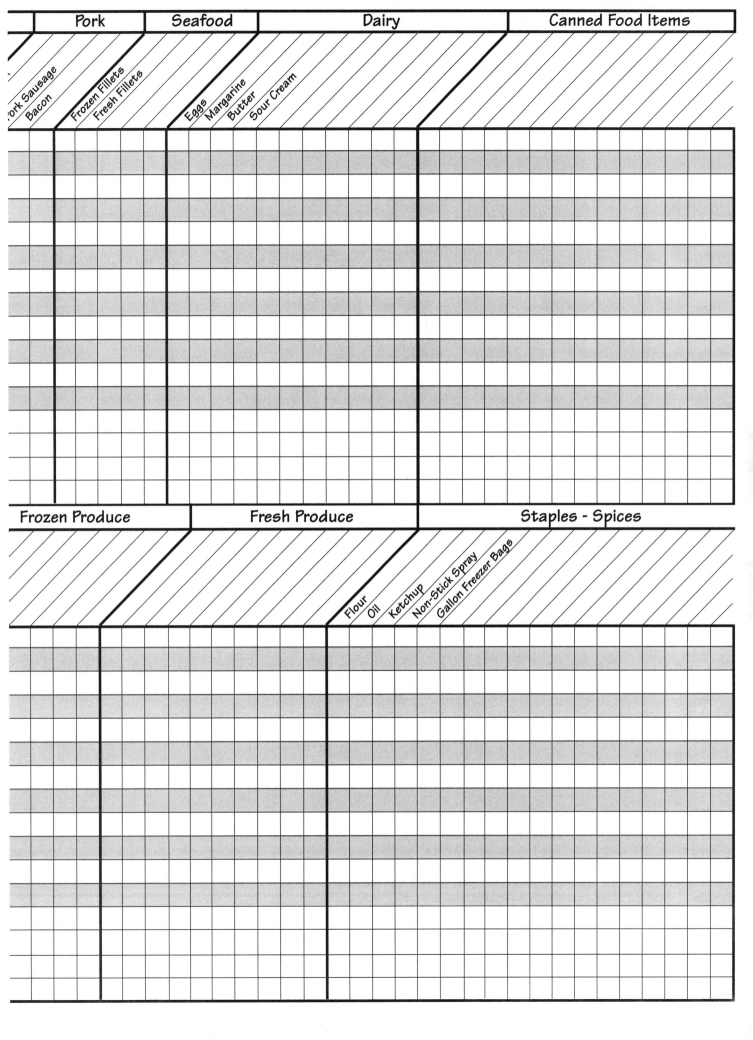

		Pork			Seafood				Dairy								Canned Food Items						

Pork Sausage · Bacon · Frozen Fillets · Fresh Fillets · Eggs · Margarine · Butter · Sour Cream

	Frozen Produce			Fresh Produce			Staples - Spices						

Flour · Oil · Ketchup · Non-Stick Spray · Gallon Freezer Bags

Planning Worksheets

BEEF	CANNED GOODS	FROZEN FOODS	OILS
CHICKEN			**MIXES**
TURKEY		**FRESH PRODUCE**	**STAPLES**
PORK	**GRAINS**		
FISH	**PASTA**		
DAIRY	**BREADS**	**SPICES**	**MISCELLANEOUS**

Planning Worksheets

What To Do Before Assembly Day	
Cook #1	Cook #2

What To Bring On Assembly Day	
Cook # 1	Cook #2

Planning

Meal Inventory Checklist
Date_____

# Of Recipes Stored						Recipe	Needed On-Hand For Serving

Be sure to place a slash in a box as a recipe goes into the freezer, then cross one off as it comes out to be served. You can use this list for foods other than your **30 Day Gourmet** recipes to help you keep track of what might be lurking in the back corner!

Planning Worksheets

MONTHLY MENU PLANNER - WORKSHEET G   MONTH _____

Saturday					
Friday					
Thursday					
Wednesday					
Tuesday					
Monday					
Sunday					

Recipes

Recipes - What our cooks say:

Yummy Cookies

Just a note to say thank you. My husband just tried the Oatmeal Chocolate Chip Cookies and in his words . . . These are not just good, they're GREAT!!!!!! Now I can have cookies on the go in the freezer to make up as needed to fix that 11:00 pm sweet tooth craving and it also stops him going out late at night to bring home extra junk food!

Sue
Traverse City, MI

Seniors Love 'Em

Our kids are all grown and gone but this is a grea way to cook for the two of us. Your book taught me a lot about freezing food in small portions for great taste. I also love having a couple of large entrees for company. Good recipes!

Mary Ann
Pine Grove, CA

Just Perfect!

I just received my 30 Day Gourmet cookbook and I am looking thru it on my lunch hour in my office! It is exactly what I was looking for! Most of the other freezer meals cookbooks have too many fancy ingredients. This is perfect for my family of 5. Thank you so much!

Michelle
Midland, TX

Saving Time and Money

We just tried your Crispy Rice Chicken recipe. It's wonderful, easy and definitely inexpensive. I have adopted your tips for shopping once monthly and freezing meals ahead of time. It has saved me lots of time and expense. Thnaks!

Camille
Rochester, NY

Love every recipe

We finished the day with 41 meals each and a huge sense of accomplishment and joy knowing that for the next 6 weeks we wouldn't have to worry about dinner. Thanks to both of you so much for showing us this fun way to make our lives easier. And to our delight and surprise our families have loved EVERY recipe. Thanks, too, for the additional recipes on your website. It's great to buy a cookbook and continue to get recipes and support. Thanks again from two moms with more time on their hands.

Jody and Cheryl
San Jose, CA

Eating well and saving money

Most of my friends thought I was nuts trying to cook for a month or more in advance, but they have changed their minds when they saw how well we are eating. We have saved hundreds of dollars as well. Thank you for sharing this great idea.

Mary Ann
Harrisburg, PA

Family of 7 loves the recipes

This system is fantastic! The charts and organization is the best ever! The recipes are ones that my husband, five kids and myself have enjoyed. Now I have more time for all of their activities without the worry of what's for dinner.

Cyndy
West Palm Beach

Beef Recipes

- Lazy Day Lasagna

- Master Meat Mix with Meatballs & Meatloaf

- Cheeseburger Quiche

- Mexican Meat Filling

- Master Beef Cube Mix

- Pizza Burgers

- Zippy Spaghetti Sauce

- Make-Ahead Beef Chimichangas

- Marinades for Beef

- Swiss Steak

Beef Recipes

TIPS FOR BEEF RECIPES

General Tips for Beef

- One pound of fresh ground beef will yield approximately 2-1/2 cups of browned beef.
- 1/4 pound of fresh beef is considered to be a standard serving.
- 2 ounces of lean red meat is considered to be a standard serving.
- Use a cookie scoop with a spring mechanism to form meatballs. Much quicker!
- Boil your ground beef to easily cook large quantities.
- When purchasing beef from the supermarket, avoid the leaking packages and place the beef on the bottom of the cart so that if there are meat juice drips, they don't drip on your other foods!
- If you purchase meats on sale to save up for your next Assembly Day, add more freezer quality wrap to your packages. Grocery store packaging is permeable to air and isn't designed for long term storage.
- Remember that if you buy ahead and freeze beef, you should cook it thoroughly before re-freezing.
- Ground beef should be heated to a temperature of at least 160 degrees F to be considered safe to eat, no matter what kind of dish it is in or how it is prepared. Thoroughly cooked ground beef will have no pink left in the middle or in juices.
- Purchase beef that is as fresh as possible. The quality will not improve in the freezer, so start with the best quality you can afford.
- Remember to cool your cooked meats before you freeze them.
- For the best quality and safety of your freezer meals, do not freeze more than 3 pounds of fresh foods per cubic foot of freezer space at one time.
- What to choose? I used to call Tara from the grocery store when buying beef. So many choices. So many sales. What to buy? Here are some general guidelines:

    Uncooked ground beef recipes: buy the best you can afford.

Cooked ground beef recipes: Cheaper is okay. Drain and rinse if you want to lower the fat content.

Stew beef recipes: Buy pre-cut and packaged for a faster prep time. If stew beef isn't on sale, you can check prices on any beef chuck or round cut (except top round) and cut it yourself.

Steaks: The more tender the cut, the better they will taste when cooked by dry-heat (grill, broil, stir-fry). The best tender steaks include top loin, T-Bone, Porterhouse, rib-eye and tenderloin. Less expensive but still tender steaks include shoulder center, top sirloin, top blade, chuck eye and round tip.

- Check out www.itswhatsfordinner.com for lots of great info on beef.

Healthy Tips for Beef

- Nutritional information for our ground beef recipes are based on using ground round which is 15% fat. For less fat in your recipes, you may choose ground sirloin (10% fat) or lean ground beef (8% fat).
- If you want to pay the cheaper prices for ground beef but have the benefits of less fat, try rinsing the fat off your cooked ground beef. Place the hot, cooked ground meat in a colander in your sink with a pan under the colander. Catch all possible fat in the pan and discard. After the meat has drained, pour hot water over the meat in the colander to remove remaining surface fat. Continue to run the hot water so that the fat runs through your drain easily and does not clog in the pipes. Allow the water to drain well from the beef before using it.
- Using the Drain and Rinse method will give you the same fat and caloric content as the leanest ground beef. Contrary to popular opinion, you don't lose so much weight with the fat that the cheaper beef isn't as "cost efficient".
- A low fat and economical alternative to using ground beef is ground turkey. I buy ground turkey for .77 a pound. It doesn't taste exactly like beef (maybe because it isn't) but you can get used to the taste or you can try mixing it with your beef.

Recipe: Lazy Day Lasagna

Recipes:	1	2	3	4	5	6
Servings:	12	24	36	48	60	72
Makes: 9"x13" pan or 2-8"x8"	1	2	3	4	5	6
Ingredients:						
Cottage cheese	12 oz.	24 oz.	36 oz.	48 oz.	60 oz.	72 oz.
Shredded mozzarella cheese	2 C.	4 C.	6 C.	8 C.	10 C.	12 C.
Eggs	2	4	6	8	10	12
Chopped parsley	1/3 C.	2/3 C.	1 C.	1-1/3 C.	1-2/3 C.	2 C.
Onion powder	1 t.	2 t.	1 T.	1 T. + 1 t.	1 T. + 2 t.	2 T.
Dried basil leaves	1/2 t.	1 t.	1-1/2 t.	2 t.	2-1/2 t.	1 T.
Pepper	1/8 t.	1/4 t.	1/4 t. + 1/8 t.	1/2 t.	1/2 t. + 1/8 t.	3/4 t.
*Spaghetti sauce	32 oz.	64 oz.	96 oz.	128 oz.	160 oz.	192 oz.
Cooked ground beef	3/4 C.	1-1/2 C.	2-1/4 C.	3 C.	3-3/4 C.	4-1/2 C.
Lasagna noodles, uncooked	9	18	27	36	45	54
**Water	3/4 C.	1-1/2 C.	2-1/4 C.	3 C.	3-3/4 C.	4-1/2 C.
On Hand:						
Grated parmesan cheese						

*Spaghetti sauce can be homemade or purchased. See our recipe for Zippy Spaghetti Sauce on page 55.

**For firmer pasta, decrease the water to 1/2 C. per recipe.

Assembly Directions:

In a large bowl, mix cottage cheese, mozzarella cheese, eggs, parsley, onion powder, basil and pepper until well blended. Set aside. In a medium bowl, mix together spaghetti sauce and cooked ground beef. In a 9"x13" glass baking dish, spread 3/4 C. meat sauce on the bottom. Layer 3 uncooked noodles on top of the meat sauce. Next spread 1/2 of cheese mixture and 1-1/2 C. meat sauce. Layer 3 more uncooked noodles on top of the meat sauce. Spread with remaining cheese mixture. Top with remaining 3 noodles and remaining meat sauce. Pour water around the outside edges.

Freezing Directions:

Place dish in a 2-gallon freezer bag. Or, if you want to wrap it in foil, cover the top of the lasagna with wax paper or plastic wrap and then the foil, because the acid in the tomato sauce will leave small holes in the foil. Label, seal and freeze.

Serving Directions:

Remove pan from freezer and thaw at least overnight in the refrigerator. Bake covered at 375 degrees for 45 minutes. Uncover and bake an additional 15 minutes. Let stand 10 minutes. Serve with grated Parmesan cheese, if desired. To bake from the frozen stage, add 30 minutes to the total baking time.

Nutritional Info: Lazy Day Lasagna

A meatless spaghetti sauce was used for the nutritional analysis.

Per Serving: 233 Calories; 10g Fat (37.3% calories from fat);
15g Protein; 21g Carbohydrate; 2g Dietary Fiber; 58mg Cholesterol; 554mg Sodium.
Exchanges: 1-1/2 Grain (Starch); 1-1/2 Lean Meat; 1 Fat.

Nutritional information for a "lite" version of this recipe is available on page 139.

BEEF RECIPES

Recipe: Master Meat Mix

Recipes:	1	2	3	4	5	6
Servings:	6	12	18	24	30	36
Makes: pans or meatballs	1/30	2/60	3/90	4/120	5/150	6/180
Ingredients:						
Lean ground beef	1-1/2 lbs.	3 lbs.	4-1/2 lbs.	6 lbs.	7-1/2 lbs.	9 lbs.
Oats, uncooked	2/3 C.	1-1/3 C.	2 C.	2-2/3 C.	3-1/3 C.	4 C.
Diced onion	1/2 C.	1 C.	1-1/2 C.	2 C.	2-1/2 C.	3 C.
Salt	1 t.	2 t.	1 T.	1 T. + 1 t.	1 T. + 2 t.	2 T.
Garlic powder	1/2 t.	1 t.	1-1/2 t.	2 t.	2-1/2 t.	1 T.
Eggs	2	4	6	8	10	12
Ketchup or tomato sauce	2/3 C.	1-1/3 C.	2 C.	2-2/3 C.	3-1/3 C.	4 C.

Assembly Directions:
Put ground beef, oats, onion, salt, garlic powder, eggs and ketchup in a large bowl. Mix together well with your hands.
Meatloaf: go on to freezing directions.
Meatballs: Form meatballs with your hands or a small cookie scoop. Cover a rimmed baking sheet with foil for easy clean-up. Put the raw meatballs on the baking sheet. Bake at 375 degrees for 20-30 minutes, until lightly browned and no longer pink in the center. Cool.

Freezing Directions:
Meatloaf: Put the meat mixture in a 1-gallon freezer bag. Seal, label and freeze.
Meatballs: Package the cooled meatballs in the appropriate size freezer bag(s) or rigid container(s) based on your family size. Seal, label and freeze.

Serving Directions:
Meatloaf: Thaw. Dump the meat mixture into a loaf pan and pack it down. Bake at 350 degrees for 1 hour or until no pink shows in the center. Cool 10 minutes before slicing and serving.
Meatballs: Thaw. Bake at 350 degrees for 10-20 minutes until hot. If you are serving the meatballs with a sauce, put them in a baking dish and pour the sauce over them. Bake at 350 degrees for 20-30 minutes, turning the meatballs occasionally while they are cooking. Serve as is, or over rice, pasta or potatoes, or make meatball subs.

Comments:
For some great-tasting sauce recipes and suggestions, visit the Members' section of our website at www.30daygourmet.com

Nutritional Info: Master Meat Mix
Per Serving: 389 Calories; 22g Fat (51.5% calories from fat);
27g Protein; 20g Carbohydrate; 2g Dietary Fiber; 141mg Cholesterol; 766mg Sodium.
Exchanges: 1 Grain (Starch); 3 1/2 Lean Meat; 2 1/2 Fat; 1/2 Other Carbohydrates.

Recipe: Cheeseburger Quiche

Recipes:	1	2	3	4	5	6
Servings:	6	12	18	24	30	36
Ingredients:						
Mayonnaise or salad dressing	1/2 C.	1 C.	1-1/2 C.	2 C.	2-1/2 C.	3 C.
Milk	1/2 C.	1 C.	1-1/2 C.	2 C.	2-1/2 C.	3 C.
Eggs	2	4	6	8	10	12
Cornstarch	1 T.	2 T.	3 T.	1/4 C.	1/4 C. + 1 T.	1/4 C. + 2 T.
Shredded cheddar cheese	1-1/2 C	3 C.	4-1/2 C.	6 C.	7-1/2 C.	9 C.
Diced onion	2 T.	1/4 C.	1/4 C. + 2 T.	1/2 C.	1/2 C. + 2 T.	3/4 C.
Cooked ground beef	2-1/2 C.	5 C.	7-1/2 C.	10 C.	12-1/2 C.	15 C.
**Unbaked pie shell, on hand	1	2	3	4	5	6

**- See our recipe for Freezer Pie Crusts on page 118.

Assembly Directions:
In a medium bowl blend the mayonnaise, milk, eggs and cornstarch. Fold in the cheese, onion and cooked ground beef.

Freezing Directions:
Pour the filling for each recipe in a 1-gallon freezer bag. Seal, label and freeze. Keep the pie crust in the freezer or refrigerator, based on when you plan to serve it.

Serving Directions:
Thaw the filling at least overnight in the refrigerator. Thaw the pie shell, if necessary. Pour the filling into the pie crust. Bake at 350 degrees for 35 to 40 minutes or until a knife inserted in the center comes out wet but clean.

Comments:
You can bake this quiche and then freeze it, if you'd prefer. Place a piece of wax paper on top of the baked and cooled quiche. Wrap completely in heavy-duty aluminum foil, or put baked quiche in a 2-gallon freezer bag. To serve, thaw completely and then reheat at 350 degrees for 20 minutes. You can also replace the ground beef with 2 C. diced raw broccoli or 2 C. diced ham or 2 C. cooked ground sausage.

Nutritional Info: Cheeseburger Quiche
Per Serving: 579 Calories; 45g Fat (69.8% calories from fat);
28g Protein; 16g Carbohydrate; 1g Dietary Fiber; 153mg Cholesterol; 547mg Sodium.
Exchanges: 1 Grain (Starch); 3-1/2 Lean Meat; 5 Fat.

Nutritional Info: Cheeseburger Quiche Lite
Replace mayonnaise with imitation light, 2% milk with skim milk and cheddar cheese with low fat cheddar.
Per Serving: 414 Calories; 26g Fat (56.2% calories from fat);
26g Protein; 19g Carbohydrate; 1g Dietary Fiber; 129mg Cholesterol; 547mg Sodium.
Exchanges: 1 Grain (Starch); 3-1/2 Lean Meat; 3-1/2 Fat.

Nutritional Information for recipe variations may be found at the Members' section of our website at
www.30daygourmet.com.

Recipe: Mexican Meat Filling

Recipes:	1	2	3	4	5	6
Servings:	6	12	18	24	30	36
Ingredients:						
Lean ground beef	1-1/2 lb.	3 lbs.	4-1/2 lbs.	6 lbs.	7-1/2 lbs.	9 lbs.
Diced onion	1 C.	2 C.	3 C.	4 C.	5 C.	6 C.
Taco seasoning packet	1	2	3	4	5	6
Crushed tomatoes	16 oz.	32 oz.	48 oz.	64 oz.	80 oz.	96 oz.

Assembly Directions:

Brown the ground beef and add the onion while it's cooking. Drain any grease. Add the seasoning and tomatoes to the skillet and stir to mix. Simmer if desired, to the preferred thickness. Cool.

Freezing Directions:

Put meat mixture in a quart freezer bag or rigid container. Seal, label and freeze.

Serving Directions:

Thaw at least overnight in the refrigerator. Heat on the stovetop or in the microwave. Serve with your choice of lettuce, tomatoes, sour cream and shredded cheddar cheese for tacos, burritos, taco salad or nachos. Or use the filling for enchiladas.

Comments:

This stuff is great! Very versatile! For more nutrition, or to stretch it farther, add up to 2 C. cooked white or brown rice to each recipe.

Nutritional Info: Mexican Meat Filling

Per Serving: 293 Calories; 16g Fat (48.7% calories from fat);
26g Protein; 11g Carbohydrate; 2g Dietary Fiber; 79mg Cholesterol; 555mg Sodium.
Exchanges: 3 1/2 Lean Meat; 1 1/2 Vegetable; 1 Fat.

Nutritional Info: Mexican Meat Filling Lite

Replace lean ground beef with ground turkey.
Per Serving: 221 Calories; 10g Fat (39.6% calories from fat);
22g Protein; 11g Carbohydrate; 2g Dietary Fiber; 90mg Cholesterol; 595mg Sodium.
Exchanges: 2 1/2 Lean Meat; 1 1/2 Vegetable.

Recipe: Master Beef Cube Mix

Recipes:	1	2	3	4	5	6
Servings:	15	30	45	60	75	90
Makes:	15 C.	30 C.	45 C.	60 C.	75 C.	90 C.
Ingredients:						
Lean stew beef	5 lbs.	10 lbs.	15 lbs.	20 lbs.	25 lbs.	30 lbs.
Onion soup mix	1 packet	2 packets	3 packets	4 packets	5 packets	6 packets
Bay leaves	2	4	6	8	10	12
*Beef flavored white sauce	6 C.	12 C.	18 C.	24 C.	30 C.	36 C.
Minced mushrooms	1/4 C.	1/2 C.	3/4 C.	1 C.	1-1/4 C.	1-1/2 C.
Minced celery	1/4 C.	1/2 C.	3/4 C.	1 C.	1-1/4 C.	1-1/2 C.
Water	2 C.	4 C.	6 C.	8 C.	10 C.	12 C.
White sauce, chicken flavored Or Canned cream of chicken or mushroom soup	6 C. or 42 oz.	12 C. or 84 oz.	18 C. or 126 oz.	24 C. or 168 oz.	30 C. or 210 oz.	36 C. or 252 oz.

*- See our White Sauce recipe on page 108.

Assembly Directions:
Combine beef, soup mix, bay leaves, white sauce or canned soup, mushrooms, celery and water in a large Dutch oven or covered roasting pan. Stir well. Bake at 300 degrees for about 4 hours, or until meat is tender. Allow mixture to cool. Discard bay leaves.

Freezing Directions:
Measure 5 C. cooled mixture into gallon freezer bags. Seal, label and freeze.

Serving Directions:
Thaw at least overnight in the refrigerator. Heat on stove top or in the microwave. Serve over pasta, rice or potatoes.

Comments:
Recipes for using this Beef Cube mix to make Cowboy Stew, Beef Stroganoff, and Beef Pot Pie are available in the Members' section of our website at www.30daygourmet.com. Nutritional information for these variations may be found there as well.

Nutritional Info: Master Beef Cube Mix
Per Serving: 423 Calories; 22g Fat (47.8% calories from fat); 43g Protein; 11g Carbohydrate; 1g Dietary Fiber; 103mg Cholesterol; 594mg Sodium.
Exchanges: 1/2 Grain(Starch); 5-1/2 Lean Meat; 1/2 Non-Fat Milk; 2 Fat.

Nutritional Info: Master Beef Cube Mix - Lite
Replace White Sauce with Fat Free White Sauce.
Per Serving: 335 Calories; 11g Fat (31.1% calories from fat); 43g Protein; 13g Carbohydrate; 1g Dietary Fiber; 97mg Cholesterol; 489mg Sodium.
Exchanges: 1/2 Grain(Starch); 5-1/2 Lean Meat; 1/2 Non-Fat Milk.

Recipe: Pizza Burgers

Recipes:	1	2	3	4	5	6
Servings:	24	48	72	96	120	144
Ingredients:						
Cooked ground beef	2-1/2 C.	5 C.	7-1/2 C.	10 C.	12-1/2 C.	15 C.
Pizza sauce	30 oz.	45 oz.	60 oz.	75 oz.	90 oz.	105 oz.
Garlic salt	1/2 t.	1 t.	1-1/2 t.	2 t.	2-1/2 t.	1 T.
Onion salt	1/2 t.	1 t.	1-1/2 t.	2 t.	2-1/2 t.	1 T.
Oregano	1/4 t.	1/2 t.	3/4 t.	1 t.	1-1/4 t.	1-1/2 t.
Pepperoni, cut into small pieces	3 oz.	6 oz.	9 oz.	12 oz.	15 oz.	18 oz.
Shredded mozzarella cheese	2 C.	4 C.	6 C.	8 C.	10 C.	12 C.
Hamburger buns	24	48	72	96	120	144

Assembly Directions:
In a large bowl, mix the ground beef, pizza sauce, garlic salt, onion salt and oregano. Add the pepperoni pieces and mozzarella cheese, stirring to mix well. Fill buns with meat mixture. Wrap each bun in aluminum foil.

Freezing Directions:
Put all of the wrapped buns in a rigid container or 2-gallon freezer bag. Seal, label and freeze.

Serving Directions:
Remove the number of wrapped buns you need from the freezer. Allow them to thaw, still wrapped in foil, for no more than an hour. (If they thaw for too long, the buns will get soggy.) Bake the wrapped buns at 350 degrees for 15-20 minutes. Serve while hot.

Comments:
These pizza burgers make a great snack too. If you are used to eating pizza burgers open-faced, you can do that with this recipe too. Freeze the mixture in freezer bags, according to your family size and appetite. To serve, thaw the mixture, and spread it on both halves of the hamburger buns. Put the halves on a cookie sheet. Broil the pizza burgers until they're hot and bubbly.

Nutritional Info: Pizza Burgers
Per Serving: 256 Calories; 11g Fat (40.3% calories from fat);
13g Protein; 25g Carbohydrate; 1g Dietary Fiber; 32mg Cholesterol; 647mg Sodium.
Exchanges: 1 1/2 Grain (Starch); 1 1/2 Lean Meat; 1/2 Vegetable; 1 1/2 Fat.

Nutritional Info: Pizza Burgers Lite
Replace ground round with ground turkey and mozzarella with low fat mozzarella.
Per Serving: 232 Calories; 9g Fat (34.0% calories from fat);
11g Protein; 27g Carbohydrate; 1g Dietary Fiber; 26mg Cholesterol; 683mg Sodium.
Exchanges: 1 1/2 Grain (Starch); 1 Lean Meat; 1/2 Vegetable; 1 Fat.

Recipe: Zippy Spaghetti Sauce

Recipes:	1	2	3	4	5	6
Servings:	6	12	18	24	30	36
Makes:	6 C.	12 C.	18 C.	24 C.	30 C.	36 C.
Ingredients:						
Cooked lean ground beef	2-1/2 C.	5 C.	7-1/2 C.	10 C.	12-1/2 C.	15 C.
Diced onion	1/2 C.	1 C.	1-1/2 C.	2 C.	2-1/2 C.	3 C.
Minced garlic	2 t.	1 T. + 1 t.	2 T.	2 T. + 2 t.	3 T. + 1 t.	1/4 C.
Minced green pepper (optional)	1/2 C.	1 C.	1-1/2 C.	2 C.	2-1/2 C.	3 C.
Tomato sauce	8 oz.	16 oz.	24 oz.	32 oz.	40 oz.	48 oz.
Tomato paste	6 oz.	12 oz.	18 oz.	24 oz.	30 oz.	36 oz.
Water	1 C.	2 C.	3 C.	4 C.	5 C.	6 C.
Oregano	1 t.	2 t.	1 T.	1 T. + 1 t.	1 T. + 2 t.	2 T.
Basil	1/4 t.	1/2 t.	3/4 t.	1 t.	1-1/4 t.	1-1/2 t.
Sugar (optional)	1 t.	2 t.	1 T.	1 T. + 1 t.	1 T. + 2 t.	2 T.
Pepper	1/4 t.	1/2 t.	3/4 t.	1 t.	1-1/4 t.	1-1/2 t.

Assembly Directions:
Combine cooked ground beef, onion, garlic, green pepper (optional), tomato sauce, tomato paste, water, oregano, basil, sugar (optional) and pepper in a saucepan or slow cooker. Simmer one hour in saucepan or 6 hours to overnight on low in the slow cooker. The longer this sauce simmers, the thicker it gets. Cool completely.

Freezing Directions:
Pour cooled sauce into a 1-gallon freezer bag or a rigid container. Seal, label and freeze.

Serving Directions:
Thaw. Heat in a saucepan over medium heat, or in the microwave.

Comments:
We use this for spaghetti, lasagna, goulash, manicotti, cheese-filled shells and any other recipe that calls for spaghetti sauce! All these meals are that much easier if you have the sauce pre-made!

Nutritional Info: Zippy Spaghetti Sauce
Per Serving: 210 Calories; 11g Fat (44.8% calories from fat);
18g Protein; 11g Carbohydrate; 2g Dietary Fiber; 53mg Cholesterol; 499mg Sodium.
Exchanges: 2 1/2 Lean Meat; 2 Vegetable; 1/2 Fat.

Nutritional Info: Zippy Spaghetti Sauce without Meat
Per Serving: 48 Calories; trace Fat (4.8% calories from fat);
2g Protein; 11g Carbohydrate; 2g Dietary Fiber; 0mg Cholesterol; 455mg Sodium.
Exchanges: 2 Vegetable.

Recipe: Make-ahead Chimichangas

Recipes:	1	2	3	4	5	6
Servings:	16	32	48	64	80	96
Ingredients:						
Cooked ground beef	2-1/2 C.	5 C.	7-1/2 C.	10 C.	12-1/2 C.	15 C.
Salsa, as spicy as you like	16 oz.	32 oz.	48 oz.	64 oz.	80 oz.	96 oz.
Refried beans	16 oz.	32 oz.	48 oz.	64 oz.	80 oz.	96 oz.
Taco seasoning envelope	1	2	3	4	5	6
8" flour tortillas	16	32	48	64	80	96
Shredded cheddar cheese	4 C.	8 C.	12 C.	16 C.	20 C.	24 C.

Assembly Directions:

In a pan, combine beef, salsa, beans and seasoning envelope. Cook and stir over medium heat until heated through. Heat a non-stick skillet on medium-low and spray with cooking spray. One at a time put the tortillas in the skillet, heating for about 30 seconds on each side. Put 1/2 C. meat mixture on each heated tortilla and top with some cheese. Fold in the sides and then roll it up.

Freezing Directions:

Wrap each rolled tortilla in foil, plastic wrap or a sandwich baggie. Put the individually wrapped Chimichangas in a freezer bag or rigid container. Seal, label and freeze.

Serving Directions:

Remove the needed amount of Chimichangas from the freezer. If they're wrapped in plastic wrap or a baggie, remove and discard the wrap/baggie. If they're wrapped in foil, you can leave the foil on to reheat. Bake at 350 degrees for 30-40 minutes. Serve with sour cream if desired.

Comments:

Vary this recipe based on your family's preference. Cooked, shredded chicken and Monterey Jack cheese taste great too. If you prefer a crispier shell, you can fry the Chimichangas instead of baking them.

Nutritional Info: Make Ahead Chimichanges (baked not fried)
Per Serving: 454 Calories; 19g Fat (37.4% calories from fat);
22g Protein; 49g Carbohydrate; 4g Dietary Fiber; 50mg Cholesterol; 943mg Sodium.
Exchanges: 3 Grain (Starch); 2 Lean Meat; 1/2 Vegetable; 2 1/2 Fat

Nutritional Info: Make-Ahead Chimichangas Lite
Replace ground round with ground turkey and cheddar cheese with low fat cheddar cheese.
Per Serving: 371 Calories; 10g Fat (24.1% calories from fat);
20g Protein; 49g Carbohydrate; 4g Dietary Fiber; 28mg Cholesterol; 951mg Sodium.
Exchanges: 3 Grain (Starch); 1 1/2 Lean Meat; 1/2 Vegetable; 1 Fat

Recipe: Beef in Marinade

Recipes:	1	2	3	4	5	6
Servings:	**6**	**12**	**18**	**24**	**30**	**36**
Makes:	**3 C.**	**6 C.**	**9 C.**	**12 C.**	**15 C.**	**18 C.**
Ingredients:						
*Beef	2 lbs.	4 lbs.	6 lbs.	8 lbs.	10 lbs.	12 lbs.
Lemon juice	1/3 C.	2/3 C.	1 C.	1-1/3 C.	1-2/3 C.	2 C.
Worcestershire sauce	1/4 C.	1/2 C.	3/4 C.	1 C.	1-1/4 C.	1-1/2 C.
Dry mustard	2 T.	1/4 C.	1/4 C. + 2 T.	1/2 C.	1/2 C. + 2 T.	3/4 C.
Oil, any kind	1 C.	2 C.	3 C.	4 C.	5 C.	6 C.
**Red wine vinegar	1/2 C.	1 C.	1-1/2 C.	2 C.	2-1/2 C.	3 C.
**Soy sauce, any variety	1/2 C	1 C.	1-1/2 C.	2 C.	2-1/2 C.	3 C.
Black pepper	1 T.	2 T.	3 T.	1/4 C.	1/4 C. + 1 T.	1/4 C. + 2 T.
Minced garlic	2 t.	1 T. + 1 t.	2 T.	2 T. + 2 t.	3 T. + 1 t.	1/4 C.

*- For help with choosing cuts of beef, see the Beef Tips on page 48.

**- We recommend buying these items in bulk from a restaurant supply store or warehouse club. It's incredibly cheaper and easier to use than the little bottles.

Assembly Directions:
Cut beef into strips for stir fry, pieces for kabobs, or leave whole for steaks on the grill. Combine lemon juice, Worcestershire, dry mustard, oil, vinegar, soy sauce, pepper and garlic.

Freezing Directions:
Put beef in a 1-gallon freezer bag. Pour the marinade over the meat. Seal, label and freeze.

Serving Directions:
Thaw at least overnight in the refrigerator. Grill or cook beef as desired. Discard marinade.

Comments:
Marinated meat is so great to have around! You can decide later what to do with it... the hard part is getting it into the marinade! And if you think meat that has marinated 4 hours tastes good, wait until you try meat that has marinated for 3 weeks!

Nutritional Info: Marinade for Beef
Oil has been removed from nutritional analysis.
Per Serving: 327 Calories; 19g Fat (52.2% calories from fat);
31g Protein; 7g Carbohydrate; 1g Dietary Fiber; 90mg Cholesterol; 1546mg Sodium.
Exchanges: 4 Lean Meat; 1/2 Vegetable; 1 Fat.

Recipe: Swiss Steak

RECIPES	1	2	3	4	5	6
Servings	6	12	18	24	30	36
Ingredients:						
Cubed Steak	2 lbs	4 lbs	6 lbs	8 lbs	10 lbs	12 lbs
Flour	1/3 C.	2/3 C.	1 C.	1-1/3 C.	1-2/3 C.	2 C.
Salt	1/2 t.	1 t.	1-1/2 t.	2 t.	2-1/2 t.	1 T
Diced celery	2/3 C.	1-1/3 C.	2 C.	2-2/3 C.	3 1/3 C.	4 C.
Diced onion	1/2 C.	1 C.	1 1/2 C.	2 C.	2 1/2 C.	3 C.
Diced green or red pepper	1 C.	2 C.	3 C.	4 C.	5 C.	6 C.
Condensed tomato soup	10 oz	20 oz	30 oz	40 oz	50 oz	60 oz
Water	3/4 C.	1-1/2 C.	2-1/4 C.	3 C.	3-3/4 C.	4-1/2 C.
Worcestershire sauce	1 T	2 T	3 T	1/4 C.	1/4 C. + 1 T	1/4 C. + 2 T

Assembly Directions:

Mix the flour and salt. Coat the meat on both sides with the flour and place in a gallon freezer bag or rigid container and set aside. Sauté or steam the celery, onion, and peppers until tender. Mix the sautéed vegetables with the soup, water and Worcestershire sauce. Put the sauce in a quart freezer bag or rigid container.

Freezing Directions:

Seal, label and freeze both of the bags or containers.

Serving Directions:

Thaw both bags or containers at least overnight in the refrigerator. This recipe can be baked in the oven, microwave or crock pot. Spray a casserole dish with cooking spray. Put 1/2 C. sauce in the bottom of the dish, and alternate layers of meat and sauce, pouring all the extra sauce over the meat. Cover and bake at 350 degrees for 45-60 minutes, until meat is tender and no longer pink in the center. OR microwave on high for 10 minutes and then on medium for 35-40 minutes, until meat is tender and no longer pink in the center. If your microwave doesn't have a turntable, be sure to turn the pan several times during cooking. OR layer sauce and meat as above in the crock pot and cook on low for 6-8 hours until the meat is tender and no longer pink in the center.

Comments:

This dish microwaves well, with the meat coming out very tender. Surprisingly, it seems to be least tender when baked in the oven. If your kids hate the veggies, either puree them in the blender/food processor or leave them in large, one-inch chunks that can be easily picked out.

Nutritional Info: Swiss Steak

Per Serving: 379 Calories; 21g Fat (49.6% calories from fat); 32g Protein; 15g Carbohydrate; 1g Dietary Fiber; 94mg Cholesterol; 558mg Sodium.

Exchanges: 1/2 Grain (Starch); 4-1/2 Lean Meat; 1/2 Vegetable; 1-1/2 Fat.

Poultry Recipes

Poultry Recipes

TIPS FOR POULTRY RECIPES

General Tips for Poultry

- 2 ounces of chicken or turkey (one breast or two smaller pieces) is considered a standard serving.
- You can substitute diced turkey breast for diced chicken. The turkey is so much easier to buy, boil and bone than all those various parts. It is often the cheapest, too. Turkey meat will have a much firmer texture than chicken.
- Buy packages of specific parts rather than mixed fryer parts for recipes like *Parsley Parmesan Chicken*. It's hard to find a 3-legged bird if your 3 kids all want a leg. This also avoids the waste you have when dealing with necks and backs.
- When figuring how much cooked meat will be yielded from a whole bird, you can usually figure that one cup of meat will come from each pound of bird. A 4 pound chicken equals 4 pounds of meat. What about substitutions when a recipe calls for a whole chicken? One whole chicken = 3 whole breasts OR 6 half breasts OR 9 whole legs (thigh and drumstick), OR 12 thighs, OR 14 drumsticks.
- Don't buy leaking packages. Don't let raw meat juices run onto any other foods. Always clean surfaces, mixing bowls, utensils, and hands well after working with raw poultry.
- Poultry is often labeled as "previously frozen" which can be confusing. That means that at some point the poultry was kept below 26 degrees. According to the USDA, if you thaw the poultry in the refrigerator and use it uncooked in a recipe, you can put it back into the freezer in the raw form. This is good to know for assembling chicken in marinade as well as for other recipes.
- A large enameled or aluminum water bath canner is very useful. It will hold 2-3 turkey breasts or whole chickens. Placing a trivet or wire rack in the bottom will keep the meat from sticking.
- Heavy duty latex gloves or "chicken gloves" as we like to call them, are great for boning and handling hot meat. The meat will come off much quicker when it's hot.

- When cooking, insert a meat thermometer into the poultry to check the temperature. Poultry has completed cooking when the inserted thermometer reaches 185° F internal temperature. Or insert a fork into the thigh or breast and check the juices that flow. It is done when the juices run clear.
- When chicken is completely cooked, Salmonella germs are killed and will not cause food-borne illness. It's often the raw chicken juice that gets into other foods that can cause food poisoning.
- When marinating chicken with its skin still on as you would with wings or legs, try piercing the skin a few times with the tines of a fork. This allows the marinade to soak into the meat, resulting in more flavor.
- If you need boned poultry meat, cook it on the bone whenever possible and then remove the meat from the bones. The bones enhance the flavor of the meat.

Healthy Tips for Poultry

- Nutritional information for our poultry recipes uses skinless chicken breasts, diced chicken (mixed white and dark meat) or chicken fryer parts unless otherwise specified. Recipes also use regular mayonnaise, cream soups, white sauce and Velveeta cheese. "Lite" versions substitute reduced fat mayonaise, soups and dressings as well as fat free white sauce and light Velveeta.
- Plan for extra diced, cooked poultry to use in nutritious salads and sandwiches. Freeze in 2-cup portions.
- Use fat-free broth whenever possible. Wouldn't you rather consume your fat in hot fudge sundaes than in chicken broth?? To remove the fat from your homemade broth, chill it in the refrigerator until the fat that collects at the top is hard. Use a slotted spatula to lift it out and discard it.
- Try our fat free white sauce recipe to replace creamed soups in your own recipes. It tastes great!
- Bake or broil your chicken instead of frying it. Remove the skin or start with skinless meat. You can greatly reduce the fat just by following these two rules of thumb.

Recipe: Parsley Parmesan Chicken

Recipes:	1	2	3	4	5	6
Servings:	6	12	18	24	30	36
Ingredients:						
Italian salad dressing	1/4 C.	1/2 C.	3/4 C.	1 C.	1-1/4 C.	1-1/2 C.
Fresh fryer parts	2 lbs.	4 lbs.	6 lbs.	8 lbs.	10 lbs.	12 lbs.
Parmesan cheese, grated	1/2 C.	1 C.	1-1/2 C.	2 C.	2-1/2 C.	3 C.
Dry breadcrumbs	1/3 C.	2/3 C.	1 C.	1-1/3 C.	1-2/3 C.	2 C.
Parsley flakes	2 T.	1/4 C.	1/4 C. + 2 T.	1/2 C.	1/2 C. + 2 T.	3/4 C.
Paprika	1/2 t.	1 t.	1-1/2 t.	2 t.	2-1/2 t.	3 t.
Salt	1/2 t.	1 t.	1-1/2 t.	2 t.	2-1/2 t.	3 t.
Pepper	1/4 t.	1/4 t.	3/8 t.	1/2 t.	1/2 t. + 1/8 t.	3/4 t.

Assembly Directions:
To Pre-Bake on Cooking Day: Pour salad dressing in a large bowl. Add the chicken parts to the dressing, coating well. Cover and chill about 4 hours, or overnight. Turn chicken in the dressing occasionally.

Combine Parmesan cheese, dry breadcrumbs, parsley flakes, paprika, salt and pepper in a shallow bowl. Roll chicken one piece at a time in the crumbs, then place chicken in a greased 9x13 baking pan or on a cookie sheet. Spoon the excess dressing over the chicken. Bake at 350 degrees for 1 hour or until thickest piece is done.

To Bake on Serving Day: Pour chicken parts and salad dressing into a freezer bag. Combine the Parmesan cheese, dry bread crumbs, parsley flakes, paprika, salt and pepper and pour into a quart-sized freezer bag. Attach to the bag of chicken or put both bags into a larger freezer bag.

Freezing Directions:
Non-Baked Chicken: Seal, label, and freeze.

Pre-Baked Chicken: Remove from oven and cool. Put baked chicken pieces into a freezer bag or rigid freezer container. Label and freeze.

Serving Directions:
Non-Baked Chicken: Thaw chicken and coating. Roll pieces in coating and place in a greased 9x13 pan or on a cookie sheet. Bake at 350 degrees for 1 hour or until thickest piece is done.

Pre-Baked Chicken: Place chicken in a 9x13 baking dish or pan. Warm in a 400 degree oven for 10 minutes or until warmed through.

Comments:
Having the chicken already baked can really come in handy if you don't have an hour before dinnertime.

Nutritional Info: Parsley Parmesan Chicken
Per Serving: 337 Calories; 24g Fat (65.5% calories from fat); 23g Protein; 6g Carbohydrate; trace Dietary Fiber; 105mg Cholesterol; 509mg Sodium.

Exchanges: 1/2 Grain (Starch); 3 Lean Meat; 3 Fat.

Nutritional information for a "lite" version of this recipe may be found on page 139.

Recipe: Crispy Rice Chicken

Recipes:	1	2	3	4	5	6
Servings:	6	12	18	24	30	36
Ingredients:						
Fresh fryer parts	2 lbs.	4 lbs.	6 lbs.	8 lbs.	10 lbs.	12 lbs.
Eggs, beaten	1	2	3	4	5	6
Water	1/2 C.	1 C.	1-1/2 C.	2 C.	2-1/2 C.	3 C.
Coarsely crushed Crispy rice cereal	1-1/2 C.	3 C.	4-1/2 C.	6 C.	7-1/2 C	9 C.
Garlic powder	1/2 t.	1 t.	1-1/2 t.	2 t.	2-1/2 t.	3 t.
Salt	1/2 t.	1 t.	1-1/2 t.	2 t.	2-1/2 t.	3 t.
Pepper	1/4 t.	1/2 t.	3/4 t.	1 t.	1-1/4 t.	1-1/2 t.

Assembly Directions:

To Pre-Bake on Cooking Day: Rinse and pat dry fryer parts. Beat the egg and water together in a shallow bowl. Place cereal crumbs in another shallow bowl and mix in the garlic powder, salt, and pepper. Dip the fryer parts in the egg mixture, then roll in the crumb mixture to coat all sides. Place each piece in a spray treated or foil-lined 9x13 baking pan, or shallow baking dish. Pre-bake 45 minutes at 350 degrees or until juices run clear. Cool.

To Bake on Serving Day: Prepare chicken and coat as above. Do not bake.

Freezing Directions:

Pre-Baked Chicken: Remove from oven and cool. Put baked chicken pieces into a freezer bag or rigid container. Label and freeze.

Non-Baked Chicken: Place coated chicken in gallon freezer bags or rigid containers. Label and freeze. If using freezer bags, you may want to "open freeze" the chicken first. Place chicken on a baking sheet and place it in the freezer, uncovered, until firm. Remove and put into freezer bags. This will help keep the coating on the chicken and will keep the pieces from freezing to each other.

Serving Directions:

Pre-Baked Chicken: Place chicken in a 9x13 baking dish or pan. Finish baking at 350 degrees for 20-30 minutes until hot and browned.

Non-Baked Chicken: Thaw coated chicken pieces and place in spray treated or foil-lined 9x13 pan or shallow baking dish. Bake uncovered at 350 degrees for 1 hour.

Comments:

Having the chicken already baked can really come in handy if you don't have an hour before dinnertime.

Nutritional Info: Crispy Rice Chicken

Per Serving: 275 Calories; 18g Fat (59.9% calories from fat); 20g Protein; 7g Carbohydrate; trace Dietary Fiber; 131mg Cholesterol; 315mg Sodium.

Exchanges: 1/2 Grain (Starch); 3 Lean Meat; 2 Fat.

Nutritional information for a "lite" version of this recipe may be found on page 139.

POULTRY RECIPES

Recipe: Debbie's Chicken in Marinade

Recipes:	1	2	3	4	5	6
Servings:	6	12	18	24	30	36
Makes:	3 C.	6 C.	9 C.	12 C.	15 C.	18 C.
Ingredients:						
Boneless, skinless chicken breast halves	6	12	18	24	30	36
Salt	2 t.	1 T. + 1 t.	2 T.	2 T. + 2 t.	3 T. + 1 t.	4 T.
Worcestershire sauce	1/4 C.	1/2 C.	3/4 C.	1 C.	1-1/4 C.	1-1/2 C.
Dry mustard	2 T.	1/4 C.	1/4 C. + 2 T.	1/2 C.	1/2 C. + 2 T.	3/4 C.
Oil (any kind)	1 C.	2 C.	3 C.	4 C.	5 C.	6 C.
Red wine vinegar	1/2 C.	1 C.	1-1/2 C.	2 C.	2-1/2 C.	3 C.
Soy sauce	3/4 C.	1-1/2 C.	2-1/4 C.	3 C.	3-3/4 C.	4-1/2 C.
Pepper	1 t.	2 t.	1 T.	1 T. + 1 t.	1 T. + 2 t.	2 T.
Minced garlic	1 t.	2 t.	1 T.	1 T. + 1 t.	1 T. + 2 t.	2 T.
Parsley flakes	1-1/2 t.	1 T.	1 T. + 1-1/2 t.	2 T.	2 T. + 1-1/2 t.	3 T.

Assembly Directions:
Combine all marinade ingredients. Place the chicken pieces in 1-gallon freezer bag or rigid container. Pour marinade over the meat.

Freezing Directions:
Seal, label and freeze.

Serving Directions:
Thaw in refrigerator or in microwave. Grill or cook chicken until the meat is no longer pink inside and the juices run clear. Discard marinade.

Comments:
Great to have on hand for grilling season or anytime! (Nanci makes her husband clean snow off the grill to serve this in the winter!) This is also a wonderful company meal. Just pull out two or three bags instead of one! We usually buy Worcestershire sauce, red wine vinegar, and soy sauce in bulk from a restaurant supply store. It is incredibly cheaper and easier to use than the little bottles.
For Chicken Strips: Cut chicken breasts into strips and marinade to use for stir fry, fajitas, or hot off the grill.

Nutritional Info: Debbie's Chicken in Marinade
Oil has been removed from the nutritional analysis since very little remains on the chicken.
Per Serving: 168 Calories; 2g Fat (11% calories from fat); 30g Protein; 7g Carbohydrate; trace Dietary Fiber; 68mg Cholesterol; 2992mg Sodium.
Exchanges: 4 Lean Meat; 1/2 Vegetable.

Recipe: Italian Chicken

Recipes:	1	2	3	4	5	6
Servings:	6	12	18	24	30	36
Ingredients:						
Chicken breasts; bone in, skin removed	6	12	18	24	30	36
Italian salad dressing	8 oz.	16 oz.	24 oz.	32 oz.	40 oz.	48 oz.
Cream cheese	8 oz.	16 oz.	24 oz.	32 oz.	40 oz.	48 oz.
Chicken broth	14 oz.	28 oz.	42 oz.	56 oz.	70 oz.	84 oz.
Canned cream of chicken soup	10-1/2 oz.	21 oz.	31-1/2 oz.	42 oz.	52-1/2 oz.	63 oz.
Rosemary	1/2 t.	1 t.	1-1/2 t.	2 t.	2-1/2 t.	3 t.
Thyme	1/2 t.	1 t.	1-1/2 t.	2 t.	2-1/2 t.	3 t.
Salt and pepper to taste						
On Hand:						
Angel hair pasta (or spaghetti)	12 oz.	24 oz.	36 oz.	48 oz.	60 oz.	72 oz.

Assembly Directions:

Put the chicken breasts in a slow cooker and pour the Italian salad dressing over them. Cook on low 8-10 hours. Remove chicken breasts from slow cooker and discard Italian dressing. Put the cream cheese, chicken broth, cream of chicken soup, rosemary, thyme and salt and pepper to taste in the slow cooker. Stir together as the ingredients melt. Meanwhile, remove the chicken from the bones and cut in small pieces. Put the chicken back in the slow cooker with the sauce. Cook together another hour. Or, you can do this step on the stove to speed it up. After it has cooked together, allow it to cool.

Freezing Directions:

Place the mixture in one-gallon freezer bags or rigid freezer container. Seal, label and freeze.

Serving Directions:

Thaw in refrigerator or microwave. Prepare pasta according to package directions. Warm the mixture in a large saucepan or in the microwave until heated through. Serve over pasta.

Comments:

Kids and adults both love this meal! It's very easy too! You can use boneless, skinless chicken breasts in place of bone-in chicken breasts if you prefer. Cook on low 5-6 hours.

Nutritional Info: Italian Chicken

Per Serving: 504 Calories; 37g Fat (66.3% calories from fat); 33g Protein; 9g Carbohydrate; trace Dietary Fiber; 114mg Cholesterol; 1119mg Sodium.

Exchanges: 1/2 Grain (Starch); 4-1/2 Lean Meat; 1/2 Fruit; 7 Fat.

Nutritional information for a "lite" version of this recipe may be found on page 139.

Recipe: Country Chicken Pot Pie

Recipes:	1	2	3	4	5	6
Servings:	12	24	36	48	60	72
Makes: pies	2	4	6	8	10	12
Ingredients:						
Chopped onions	1 C.	2 C.	3 C.	4 C.	5 C.	6 C.
Chopped celery	1 C.	2 C.	3 C.	4 C.	5 C.	6 C.
Chopped carrots	1 C.	2 C.	3 C.	4 C.	5 C.	6 C.
Butter/margarine, melted	1/3 C.	2/3 C.	1 C.	1-1/3 C.	1-2/3 C.	2 C.
Flour	1/2 C.	1 C.	1-1/2 C.	2 C.	2-1/2 C.	3 C.
Chicken broth	2 C.	4 C.	6 C.	8 C.	10 C.	12 C.
Evaporated milk	1 C.	2 C.	3 C.	4 C.	5 C.	6 C.
Chicken; cooked & chopped	4 C.	8 C.	12 C.	16 C.	20 C.	24 C.
Frozen peas, thawed	1 C.	2 C.	3 C.	4 C.	5 C.	6 C.
Salt	1-1/2 t.	1 T.	1 T. + 1-1/2 t.	2 T.	2 T. + 1-1/2 t.	3 T.
Pepper	1/4 t.	1/2 t.	3/4 t.	1 t.	1-1/4 t.	1-1/2 t.
Pie crusts; folded Pillsbury type	4	8	12	16	20	24

Assembly Directions:

Sauté onions, celery and carrots in butter in a large skillet over medium heat until tender. Add flour and stir until smooth. Cook one minute, stirring constantly. Add chicken broth and evaporated milk. Cook, stirring constantly until thickened and bubbly. Stir in chicken, peas, salt and pepper.

Freezing Directions:

Cool and divide filling in half. Place in one-gallon freezer bags. Seal, label and freeze. Keep frozen pie crusts on hand in their original packaging.

Serving Directions:

Thaw filling. Bring pie crusts to room temperature. Shape bottom pie crusts. Add filling. Cover with top crust. Pinch the edges of the two crusts together and then flute or crimp. Make a few slits in the top crust for the steam to escape.
Bake uncovered for 30 minutes at 350 degrees. Then bake covered with foil for 30 more minutes. Let stand 10 minutes before serving.

Nutritional Info: Country Chicken Pot Pie

Per Serving: 467 Calories; 25g Fat (49.0% calories from fat); 22g Protein; 37g Carbohydrate; 3g Dietary Fiber; 46mg Cholesterol; 926mg Sodium.
Exchanges: 2 Grain (Starch); 2 Lean Meat; 1/2 Vegetable; 4-1/2 Fat.

Recipe: Baked Chicken Fingers & Nuggets

Recipes:	1	2	3	4	5	6
Servings:	**6**	**12**	**18**	**24**	**30**	**36**
Ingredients:						
Boneless, skinless, chicken breasts	2 lbs.	4 lbs.	6 lbs.	8 lbs.	10 lbs.	12 lbs.
Sauce #1:						
Mayonnaise	1/4 C.	1/2 C.	3/4 C.	1 C.	1-1/4 C.	1-1/2 C.
Milk	1/4 C.	1/2 C.	3/4 C.	1 C.	1-1/4 C.	1-1/2 C.
Dry mustard	2 t.	1 T. + 1 t.	2 T.	2 T. + 2 t.	3 T. + 1 t.	4 T.
Onion powder	1 t.	2 t.	1 T.	1 T. + 1 t.	1 T. + 2 t.	2 T.
Sauce #2:						
Milk	1/4 C.	1/2 C.	3/4 C.	1 C.	1-1/4 C.	1-1/2 C.
Ranch dressing, bottled	1/4 C.	1/2 C.	3/4 C.	1 C.	1-1/4 C.	1-1/2 C.
Coating:						
Bread crumbs or cracker meal	1 C.	2 C.	3 C.	4 C.	5 C.	6 C.
Paprika	1/2 t.	1 t.	1-1/2 t.	2 t.	2-1/2 t.	3 t.

Assembly Directions:

Choose one sauce and then mix all the sauce ingredients together well with wire whisk, mixer, or spoon. Cut chicken breasts into lengthwise strips or nuggets. Place all of the chicken pieces in the sauce and stir well to coat. Place the coating in a plastic bag, bowl or other container with a lid. Place about one pound of chicken (or 1/2 a single recipe), in the crumb mixture. Seal container and shake well to coat pieces with crumbs. Place chicken on spray-treated or greased baking sheets and bake at 375 degrees for 15-20 minutes, turning once. Remove from oven and cool on baking sheets.

Freezing Directions:

When cool, place trays of fingers or nuggets in freezer and freeze until firm. Place frozen fingers or nuggets in freezer bags or rigid containers. Seal, label and freeze.

Serving Directions:

Place frozen fingers or nuggets on a baking sheet and reheat at 400 degrees for 5-10 minutes until hot.

Nutritional Info: Baked Chicken Fingers & Nuggets Sauce #1

Per Serving: 324 Calories; 13g Fat (36.7% calories from fat); 37g Protein; 14g Carbohydrate; 1g Dietary Fiber; 96mg Cholesterol; 293mg Sodium.

Exchanges: 1 Grain (Starch); 4-1/2 Lean Meat; 1 Fat.

Nutritional Info: Baked Chicken Fingers & Nuggets Sauce #2

Per Serving: 307 Calories; 10g Fat (31.5% calories from fat); 37g Protein; 14g Carbohydrate; trace Dietary Fiber; 95mg Cholesterol; 352mg Sodium.

Exchanges: 1 Grain (Starch); 4-1/2 Lean Meat; 1-1/2 Fat.

Nutritional information for a "lite" version of this recipe may be found on page 139.

Recipe: Chicken in a Pot

Recipes:	1	2	3	4	5	6
Servings:	6	12	18	24	30	36
Ingredients:						
Boneless, skinless chicken breasts	6	12	18	24	30	36
Italian dressing mix envelope	1	2	3	4	5	6
Cream cheese, softened	6 oz.	12 oz.	18 oz.	24 oz.	30 oz.	36 oz.
Canned cream of mushroom soup	10-1/2 oz.	21 oz.	31-1/2 oz.	42 oz.	52-1/2 oz.	63 oz.
Canned mushroom stems and pieces, drained	4 oz.	8 oz.	12 oz.	16 oz.	20 oz.	24 oz.
On Hand:						
Angel hair pasta	12 oz.	24 oz.	36 oz.	48 oz.	60 oz.	72 oz.

Assembly Directions:

Place chicken breasts in crock pot. Sprinkle dressing packet on chicken breasts in crock-pot. Do not add water! Cook on low 6-8 hrs. Then stir in rest of ingredients. Turn crock-pot to high to heat through. This should take about half an hour.

Freezing Directions:

Freeze in one-gallon freezer bag or casserole dish. Seal, label and freeze.

Serving Directions:

Thaw completely. Prepare pasta according to package directions. Heat chicken mixture in microwave till hot - about 10 minutes on 50% power. Serve over hot pasta.

Nutritional Info: Chicken in a Pot

Per Serving: 489 Calories; 15g Fat (28.4% calories from fat); 38g Protein; 48g Carbohydrate; 2g Dietary Fiber; 100mg Cholesterol; 978mg Sodium.
Exchanges: 3 Grain (Starch); 4 Lean Meat; 2-1/2 Fat.

Nutritional Info: Chicken in a Pot - Lite

Replace cream cheese with light cream cheese and cream of mushroom soup with reduced fat cream of mushroom soup.
Per Serving: 438 Calories; 8g Fat (17.3% calories from fat); 38g Protein; 50g Carbohydrate; 2g Dietary Fiber; 87mg Cholesterol; 892mg Sodium.
Exchanges: 3 Grain (Starch); 4 Lean Meat; 1 Fat.

Recipe: Chicken Spaghetti

Recipes:	1	2	3	4	5	6
Servings:	6	12	18	24	30	36
Makes:	6 C.	12 C.	18 C.	24 C.	30 C.	36 C.
Ingredients:						
Spaghetti	12 oz.	24 oz.	36 oz.	48 oz.	60 oz.	72 oz.
Boneless, skinless chicken breasts	1-1/2 lbs.	3 lbs.	4-1/2 lbs.	6 lbs.	7-1/2 lbs.	9 lbs.
Chopped onion	1-1/2 C.	3 C.	4-1/2 C.	6 C.	7-1/2 C.	9 C.
Minced garlic	1/2 t.	1 t.	1-1/2 t.	2 t.	2-1/2 t.	1 T.
Canned cream of mushroom soup	10-1/2 oz.	21 oz.	31-1/2 oz.	42 oz.	52-1/2 oz.	63 oz.
Canned cream of chicken soup	10-1/2 oz.	21 oz.	31-1/2 oz.	42 oz.	52-1/2 oz.	63 oz.
On Hand:						
Diced Velveeta cheese	2 C.	4 C.	6 C.	8 C.	10 C.	12 C.

Assembly Directions:
Cook spaghetti half the recommended time. Dice chicken into cubes and cook in small amount of water until no longer pink in the center. In a large bowl, combine chicken, onion, garlic, and soups. Add in spaghetti and thoroughly mix. Allow mixture to cool.

Freezing Directions:
Place the mixture in a one-gallon freezer bag or rigid freezer container. Seal, label and freeze.

Serving Directions:
Thaw spaghetti mixture. Mix in Velveeta cheese. Place the mixture in a casserole dish (covered). Bake at 350 degrees for 40 minutes.

Nutritional Info: Chicken Spaghetti
Per Serving: 649 Calories; 25g Fat (34.2% calories from fat); 47g Protein; 61g Carbohydrate; 2g Dietary Fiber; 121mg Cholesterol; 1845mg Sodium.
Exchanges: 3-1/2 Grain (Starch); 5 Lean Meat; 1/2 Vegetable; 3 Fat; 1/2 Other Carbohydrates.

Nutritional Info: Chicken Spaghetti - Lite
Replace cream of chicken soup with reduced fat cream of chicken soup, cream of mushroom soup with reduced fat cream of mushroom soup and Velveeta with Velveeta light.
Per Serving: 562 Calories; 13g Fat (21.1% calories from fat); 47g Protein; 62g Carbohydrate; 3g Dietary Fiber; 101mg Cholesterol; 1674mg Sodium.
Exchanges: 3 Grain (Starch); 5 Lean Meat; 1/2 Vegetable; 1/2 Fat; 1/2 Other Carbohydrates.

Recipe: Chicken Divan

Recipes:	1	2	3	4	5	6
Servings:	6	12	18	24	30	36
Ingredients:						
Cooked rice, white or brown	3 C.	6 C.	9 C.	12 C.	15 C.	18 C.
Broccoli, frozen	20 oz.	40 oz.	60 oz.	80 oz.	100 oz.	120 oz.
Lemon juice	2 T.	1/4 C.	1/4 C. + 2 T.	1/2 C.	1/2 C. + 2 T.	3/4 C.
Mayonnaise	1 C.	2 C.	3 C.	4 C.	5 C.	6 C.
Cooked, diced chicken	6 C.	12 C.	18 C.	24 C.	30 C.	36 C.
White sauce, chicken flavored Or Cream soup, canned (chicken, mushroom or broccoli)	3 C. or 21 oz.	6 C. or 42 oz.	9 C. or 63 oz.	12 C. or 84 oz.	15 C. or 105 oz.	18 C. or 126 oz.
Cheddar cheese, grated	1 C.	2 C.	3 C.	4 C.	5 C.	6 C.

Assembly Directions:

Cook the rice 3/4 the recommended time. Cook broccoli according to package directions. Set aside. Mix lemon juice and mayonnaise, then add chicken flavored white sauce or soup. Spread rice in container. Layer on broccoli, then half the sauce, then the cooked chicken, and then remaining sauce. Top with grated cheese.

Freezing Directions:

Wrap tightly with freezer paper, foil, or 2-gallon freezer bag. Seal, label and freeze.

Serving Directions:

Thaw and bake at 350 degrees for 30 minutes or until chicken is tender and easily pierced with a fork.

Comments:

We don't recommend pre-cooking this on Assembly Day since it bakes so quickly.

If it's easier, you can mix all the ingredients together except the cheese. Freeze rice, chicken, broccoli, and sauce in one bag and cheese topping in another. When ready to serve, thaw then pour into casserole. Top with cheese and bake.

Nutritional Info: Chicken Divan

Calculations were done with chicken flavored white sauce.

Per Serving: 935 Calories; 60g Fat (57.0% calories from fat); 59g Protein; 43g Carbohydrate; 3g Dietary Fiber; 168mg Cholesterol; 837mg Sodium.

Exchanges: 2 Grain (Starch); 7 Lean Meat; 1 Vegetable; 1/2 Non-Fat Milk; 6-1/2 Fat.

Nutritional Info: Chicken Divan – Lite

Replace mayonnaise with imitation reduced fat mayonnaise, white sauce with fat free white sauce and cheddar cheese with reduced fat cheddar cheese.

Per Serving: 543 Calories; 11g Fat (18.0% calories from fat); 59g Protein; 50g Carbohydrate; 4g Dietary Fiber; 142mg Cholesterol; 698mg Sodium.

Exchanges: 2 Grain (Starch); 7 Lean Meat; 1 Vegetable; 1/2 Non-Fat Milk; 1/2 Fat; 1/2 Other Carbohydrates.

Recipe: Chicken Tetrazzini

Recipes:	1	2	3	4	5	6
Servings:	12	24	36	48	60	72
Ingredients:						
White sauce, chicken flavored Or Canned cream of chicken or mushroom soup	6 C. or 42 oz.	12 C. or 84 oz.	18 C. or 126 oz.	24 C. or 168 oz.	30 C. or 210 oz.	36 C. or 252 oz.
Lemon juice	2 T.	1/4 C.	1/4 C. + 2 T.	1/2 C.	1/2 C. + 2 T.	3/4 C.
Diced green pepper (optional)	1/2 C.	1 C.	1-1/2 C.	2 C.	2-1/2 C.	3 C.
Dry spaghetti, broken in 1" pieces	4 C.	8 C.	12 C.	16 C.	20 C.	24 C.
Cooked, diced chicken	4 C.	8 C.	12 C.	16 C.	20 C.	24 C.
Mushrooms (optional)	8 oz.	16 oz.	24 oz.	32 oz.	40 oz.	48 oz.
Parmesan cheese, grated	1 C.	2 C.	3 C.	4 C.	5 C.	6 C.

Assembly Directions:

Combine white sauce or soup and lemon juice. Sauté (in a small amount of oil) or steam green pepper and add to sauce. Break spaghetti into 1" pieces and boil in salted water 1/2 the recommended time. Drain spaghetti. Mix spaghetti, chicken and mushrooms into sauce.

Optional: Cook spaghetti full recommended time and put in freezer bag. Attach to chicken and sauce. Stir into casserole just before baking.

Freezing Directions:

Pour mixture into 2-1/2 qt. casserole. Wrap in freezer paper, foil, or place pan in 2-gallon freezer bag. Seal, label and freeze. OR Pour mixture into 1-gallon freezer bag. Enclose a small freezer bag with 1 C. grated Parmesan cheese for each recipe. Seal, label and freeze.

Serving Directions:

To serve, thaw completely. Bake at 350 degrees for 45-60 minutes or until thoroughly heated. If food is in a freezer bag, thaw, pour contents into an oiled baking dish, sprinkle enclosed cheese on top, and cook as above. Frozen casserole may be baked for 1-1/2 hours at 350 degrees.

Nutritional Info: Chicken Tetrazzini

Calculations were done using white sauce, green peppers and mushrooms.
Per Serving: 431 Calories; 20g Fat (42.7% calories from fat); 26g Protein; 35g Carbohydrate; 1g Dietary Fiber; 62mg Cholesterol; 622mg Sodium.
Exchanges: 2 Grain (Starch); 2-1/2 Lean Meat; 1/2 Vegetable; 1/2 Non-Fat Milk; 3 Fat.

Nutritional Info: Chicken Tetrazzini - Lite

Replace white sauce with fat free white sauce.
Per Serving: 307 Calories; 5g Fat (15.2% calories from fat); 27g Protein; 37g Carbohydrate; 2g Dietary Fiber; 47mg Cholesterol; 492mg Sodium.
Exchanges: 2 Grain (Starch); 2-1/2 Lean Meat; 1/2 Vegetable; 1/2 Non-Fat Milk.

Pork & Fish Recipes

- Soucy Oven Pork Chops

- Marinades for Pork

- Sweet 'n Sour Kielbasa

- Seafood Lasagna

- Baked Salmon with Mustard Crumb Crust

Pork & Fish Recipes

TIPS FOR PORK & FISH RECIPES

General Tips for Pork and Fish

- 2 ounces of lean pork (Canadian bacon, tenderloin, fresh ham) is considered a serving.
- 3 ounces of tuna, crab or broiled fish is considered a standard serving.
- Most fresh fish should not have a strong "fishy" odor and the packages should not be leaking.
- Fresh fish steaks and fillets should be firm. When you lightly press on the fish with your finger, the flesh should spring back into shape.
- When choosing fish for the grill, the firmer the better. Salmon, swordfish, tuna and halibut are perfect for grilling. Steaks that are one to two inches thick work best.
- As a general rule, the lighter the color, the lighter the flavor. Sole, Pacific and Atlantic halibut, cod, flounder, grouper, sea or fresh water bass, haddock, orange roughy, and trout are some of the milder tasting fish varieties. Ling cod, snapper, whiting, perch, rockfish, bluefish, catfish, and salmon are considered to be in the moderate flavored range. Swordfish, mackerel, shad and tuna are some of the stronger flavored fish varieties.
- Generally, ten minutes of cooking time per inch of thickness is a good rule. If a fish variety is translucent (sort of clear) to begin with, it is done as soon as it is opaque (not clear). When you are sautéing fish, the pan is too hot if you can smell the fish.
- 1/4 lb. of raw fish is an adult serving.
- 1/4 C. of cooked ground pork (as in sausage) is an adult serving.
- Cured pork products (ham, bacon) should only be frozen for a month, or they will develop a strong flavor.
- You can grind your own ham in a food processor or ask your butcher to do it. When doing it yourself, cut the ham into 2" cubes and use the chopping blade. Pulse the blade until it is evenly ground.

- Pork roasts, steaks, and chops are considered medium done if the internal temperature reaches 160 degrees F. Well done roasts, steaks and chops will have a temperature of 170 degrees F.
- When choosing ribs for barbecuing, country style ribs will have quite a bit more meat on them.
- Make a cut at one-inch intervals through the fat on the edges of steaks and chops to prevent curling during cooking.
- When trying to cut thin slices, it is easier if you put the meat into the freezer for 30 minutes to an hour before slicing to help firm it up or if meat was frozen, slice before it is completely thawed.

Healthy Tips for Pork and Fish

- Nutritional information for our pork and fish recipes is based on pork loin chops and cod or Pollock fillets. Recipes use 2% milk and regular Swiss cheese. "Lite" versions substitute skim milk and lowfat Swiss cheese.
- Broil, bake, or grill fish instead of frying it in fat.
- Sole, Pacific halibut, cod, flounder, grouper, sea bass, haddock, orange roughy, ling cod, red snapper, whiting, perch, pike, and rockfish all have less than 11 grams of fat per pound.
- The higher fat fish varieties are pompano, mackerel, sablefish, and shad. These varieties all have more than 23 grams of fat per pound. Most other varieties range between 11 and 23 grams of fat per pound.
- To cut down on your red meat intake, ask the butcher to mix in an equal quantity of ground turkey with your ground pork.
- You can automatically cut out many fat grams by trimming all the visible fat from the outsides of steaks and chops.
- Boneless pork loin chops are a lower fat chop compared to other cuts, but be careful not to over-cook them or they will be very dry and chewy!

Recipe: Saucy Oven Pork Chops

Recipes:	1	2	3	4	5	6
Servings:	6	12	18	24	30	36
Ingredients:						
Pork chops	6	12	18	24	30	36
Tomato sauce, canned	15 oz.	30 oz.	45 oz.	60 oz.	75 oz.	90 oz.
Black pepper, ground	1/8 t.	1/4 t.	3/8 t.	1/2 t.	1/2 t. + 1/8 t.	3/4 t.
Salt	1/2 t.	1 t.	1-1/2 t.	2 t.	2-1/2 t.	3 t.
Dry mustard	1/2 t.	1 t.	1-1/2 t.	2 t.	2-1/2 t.	3 t.
Lemon juice	1 t.	2 t.	1 T.	1 T. + 1 t.	1 T. + 2 t.	2 T.
Water	1/2 C.	1 C.	1-1/2 C.	2 C.	2-1/2 C.	3 C.
Brown sugar	2 T.	1/4 C.	1/4 C. + 2 T.	1/2 C.	1/2 C. + 2 T.	3/4 C.
Diced celery	1/3 C.	2/3 C.	1 C.	1- 1/3 C.	1-2/3 C.	2 C.

Assembly Directions:
Coat a broiler rack or shallow pan with cooking oil and preheat the broiler. Broil the chops on the top rack until well browned. Turn them and brown the other side. Cool the chops completely. When cooled, mix all remaining ingredients together in a bowl.

Freezing Directions:
Place the cooled chops in a one-gallon freezer bag or rigid container. Pour the sauce over the chops and remove excess air. Seal, label and freeze.

Serving Directions:
Thaw the bag of chops. Pour the chops and sauce in a shallow covered baking dish. Bake at 350 degrees for 30-45 minutes or until tender.

Comments:
Great served with brown or wild rice.

Nutritional Info: Saucy Oven Pork Chops
Per Serving: 266 Calories; 15g Fat (51% calories from fat); 24g Protein; 8g Carbohydrate; 1g Dietary Fiber; 74mg Cholesterol; 673mg Sodium.
Exchanges: 3-1/2 Lean Meat; 1 Vegetable; 1 Fat.

Recipe: Marinade for Pork

Recipes:	1	2	3	4	5	6
Servings:	6	12	18	24	30	36
Makes:	3 C.	6 C.	9 C.	12 C.	15 C.	18 C.
Ingredients:						
Pork chops	6	12	18	24	30	36
Pineapple juice	16 oz.	32 oz.	48 oz.	64 oz.	80 oz.	96 oz.
*Soy sauce	1/2 C.	1 C.	1-1/2 C.	2 C.	2-1/2 C.	3 C.
Ginger, ground	1 t.	2 t.	1 T.	1 T. + 1 t.	1 T. + 2 t.	2 T.
Garlic, minced	1/2 t.	1 t.	1-1/2 t.	2 t.	2-1/2 t.	3 t.
Italian dressing	1/3 C.	2/3 C.	1 C.	1-1/3 C.	1-2/3 C.	2 C.

Assembly Directions:
Combine all marinade ingredients. Place the meat in freezer bags or containers. Pour marinade over meat.

Freezing Directions:
Seal, label and freeze.

Serving Directions:
Thaw. Grill, broil, or pan fry pork chops until browned on both sides and no longer pink in the center. Discard marinade.

Comments:
*We usually buy our soy sauce at a restaurant supply store where it is MUCH cheaper!

Nutritional Info: Marinade for Pork
Per Serving: 353 Calories; 21g Fat (54.4% calories from fat); 25g Protein; 15g Carbohydrate; trace Dietary Fiber; 74mg Cholesterol; 1534mg Sodium.
Exchanges: 3-1/2 Lean Meat; 1/2 Vegetable; 1 Fruit; 2 Fat.

Nutritional Info: Marinade for Pork - Lite
Replace Italian dressing with fat free Italian Dressing and soy sauce with reduced sodium soy sauce.
Per Serving: 299 Calories; 15g Fat (46% calories from fat); 25g Protein; 15g Carbohydrate; trace Dietary Fiber; 74mg Cholesterol; 1073mg Sodium.
Exchanges: 3-1/2 Lean Meat; 1/2 Vegetable; 1 Fruit; 1 Fat.

PORK & FISH RECIPES

Recipe: Sweet 'n Sour Kielbasa

Recipes:	1	2	3	4	5	6
Servings:	6	12	18	24	30	36
Ingredients:						
Smoked kielbasa sausage	2 lbs.	4 lbs.	6 lbs.	8 lbs.	10 lbs.	12 lbs.
Brown sugar	1 C.	2 C.	3 C.	4 C.	5 C.	6 C.
Spicy mustard	1/3 C.	2/3 C.	1 C.	1-1/3 C.	1-2/3 C.	2 C.
Finely chopped onion	1/3 C.	2/3 C.	1 C.	1-1/3 C.	1-2/3 C.	2 C.

Assembly Directions:

Cut sausages into two-inch lengths. Combine brown sugar, mustard, and onion in an electric slow cooker and stir well to combine. Add the cut sausages and stir well to coat them with the sauce. Cover the slow cooker with its lid and cook on low heat for 2-1/2 to 3 hours, stirring occasionally to re-coat the sausage with the sauce.

Freezing Directions:

Cool the sausages and sauce. Store in rigid freezer containers or freezer bags. Seal, label and freeze.

Serving Directions:

To serve, thaw and reheat in the microwave or on low heat on the stove, or in a covered dish in the oven at 350 degrees for about 15 minutes.

Comments:

This could be made with the sausage of your choice.   Kielbasa, Polish sausage, summer sausage, etc. could be used. Also, there are plenty of low-fat sausages on the market that would do well in this recipe. This recipe makes a terrific main dish, but it would also be a very nice appetizer on a casual buffet table or tailgate party recipe. The sausages would also make a nice sandwich filling on a hefty roll with some of the sauce poured over them.

Nutritional Info: Sweet and Sour Kielbasa

Per Serving: 573 Calories; 42g Fat (65.6% calories from fat); 21g Protein; 28g Carbohydrate; 1g Dietary Fiber; 101mg Cholesterol; 1805mg Sodium.
Exchanges: 3 Lean Meat; 6 Fat; 1-1/2 Other Carbohydrates.

Nutritional Info: Sweet and Sour Kielbasa – Lite

Replace kielbasa with Healthy Choices Low Fat Smoked Sausage.
Per Serving: 320 Calories; 7g Fat (21% calories from fat); 20g Protein; 41g Carbohydrate; 1g Dietary Fiber; 68mg Cholesterol; 1474mg Sodium.
Exchanges: 3 Lean Meat; 1-1/2 Fat; 1-1/2 Other Carbohydrates.

Recipe: Citrus Marinade for Fish

Recipes:	1	2	3	4	5	6
Servings:	6	12	18	24	30	36
Makes:	3/4 C.	1-1/2 C.	2-1/4 C.	3 C.	3-3/4 C.	4-1/2 C.
Ingredients:						
Fish fillets, fresh or frozen	1-1/2 lbs.	3 lbs.	4-1/2 lbs.	6 lbs.	7-1/2 lbs.	9 lbs.
Lime juice	1/3 C.	2/3 C.	1 C.	1-1/3 C.	1-2/3 C.	2 C.
Cooking oil	1 T.	2 T.	3 T.	1/4 C.	1/4 C. + 1 T.	1/4 C. + 2 T.
Salt	1/4 t.	1/2 t.	3/4 t.	1 t.	1-1/4 t.	1-1/2 t.
Water	1/3 C.	2/3 C.	1 C.	1-1/3 C.	1-2/3 C.	2 C.
Honey	1 T.	2 T.	3 T.	1/4 C.	1/4 C. + 1 T.	1/4 C. + 2 T.
Dill weed, dried	1/2 t.	1 t.	1-1/2 t.	2 t.	2-1/2 t.	3 t.

Assembly Directions:
Combine marinade ingredients.

Freezing Directions:
Pour marinade into equal freezer bags or rigid freezer containers. Seal, label and freeze. Seal fish fillets in a freezer bag and freeze.

Serving Directions:
Thaw marinade and fish until completely softened. Place thawed fish fillets in thawed marinade for 10 minutes. Remove the fish from the marinade, reserving it for later. Place fish on greased broiler rack or grill. Tuck under any thin portion. Broil 4 inches from heat element, basting often with reserved marinade, until fish flakes easily. It takes just a few minutes, so watch carefully. Brush with marinade again just before serving. Discard any leftover marinade.

Nutritional Info: Citrus Marinade for Fish
Per Serving: 127 Calories; 3g Fat (23.2% calories from fat); 20g Protein; 4g Carbohydrate; trace Dietary Fiber; 81mg Cholesterol; 202mg Sodium.
Exchanges: 2-1/2 Lean Meat; 1/2 Fat.

Recipe: Seafood Lasagna

Recipes:	1	2	3	4	5	6
Servings:	12	24	36	48	60	72
Makes: 9 x 13 pan	1	2	3	4	5	6
Ingredients:						
Lasagna noodles	12	24	36	48	60	72
Italian-style stewed tomatoes; canned, cut-up, undrained	29 oz.	58 oz.	87 oz.	116 oz.	145 oz.	174 oz.
Sliced fresh mushrooms	1/2 C.	1 C.	1-1/2 C.	2 C.	2-1/2 C.	3 C.
Onion powder	1/2 t	1 t.	1-1/2 t.	2 t.	2-1/2 t.	3 t.
Oregano	1/2 t	1 t.	1-1/2 t.	2 t.	2-1/2 t.	3 t.
Small cooked shrimp (in bite-sized pcs)	1/2 C.	1 C.	1-1/2 C.	2 C.	2-1/2 C.	3 C.
Butter or margarine	3 T.	1/4 C. + 2 T.	1/2 C. + 1 T.	3/4 C.	3/4 C. + 3 T.	1 C. + 2 T.
Flour	3 T.	1/4 C. + 2 T.	1/2 C. + 1 T.	3/4 C.	3/4 C. + 3 T.	1 C. + 2 T.
Milk	1-3/4 C.	3-1/2 C.	5-1/4 C.	7 C.	8-3/4 C.	10-1/2 C.
Shredded swiss cheese	1 C.	2 C.	3 C.	4 C.	5 C.	6 C.
Dry red wine (optional)	1/4 C.	1/2 C.	3/4 C.	1 C.	1-1/4 C.	1-1/2 C.
Imitation crab (bite-sized pcs)	8 oz.	16 oz.	24 oz.	32 oz.	40 oz.	48 oz.
On Hand:						
Grated Romano/Parmesan cheese	1/2 C.	1 C.	1-1/2 C.	2 C.	2-1/2 C.	3 C.

Assembly Directions:
Cook lasagna as package directs and drain.

To make tomato sauce: In medium saucepan, combine undrained tomatoes, mushrooms, onion powder, oregano. Salt and pepper to taste. Bring to a boil. Reduce heat and simmer uncovered 20 minutes or until thickened. Stir in shrimp. Set aside.

To make cheese sauce: In medium saucepan, melt butter. Stir in flour. Add milk, all at once, using a whisk to incorporate. Cook and stir constantly over medium heat until thickened and bubbly. Cook one minute more. Add Swiss cheese and stir until melted. Stir in wine and imitation crab.

To Assemble: In a 9 x 13 pan, layer 1/3 of the tomato sauce, a layer of noodles, and 1/3 of the cheese sauce. Repeat layers.

Freezing Directions:
Wrap tightly with freezer paper, foil or place dish in a 2-gallon bag. Seal, label and freeze.

Serving Directions:
Thaw in refrigerator 1 day before serving. Sprinkle with Romano or Parmesan cheese. Bake uncovered in a 350 degree oven for 25 minutes or until heated through. Let stand 15 minutes before serving.

Nutritional Info: Seafood Lasagna
Per Serving: 463 Calories; 9g Fat (17.6% calories from fat); 21g Protein; 72g Carbohydrate; 3g Dietary Fiber; 36mg Cholesterol; 451mg Sodium.

Exchanges: 4-1/2 Grain (Starch); 1 Lean Meat; 1/2 Vegetable; 1 Fat.

Nutritional information for a "lite" version of this recipe may be found on page 139.

Recipe: Baked Salmon with Mustard Crumb Crust

Recipes:	1	2	3	4	5	6
Servings:	4	8	12	16	20	24
Ingredients:						
Balsamic vinegar	2 T.	1/4 C.	1/4 C. + 2 T.	1/2 C.	1/2 C. + 2 T.	3/4 C.
Brown sugar	2 T.	1/4 C.	1/4 C. + 2 T.	1/2 C.	1/2 C. + 2 T.	3/4 C.
Dry mustard	1-1/2 t.	1 T.	1 T. + 1-1/2 t.	2 T.	2 T. + 1-1/2 t.	3 T.
Dijon mustard	2 T.	1/4 C.	1/4 C. + 2 T.	1/2 C.	1/2 C. + 2 T.	3/4 C.
Vegetable oil	1/3 C.	2/3 C.	1 C.	1-1/3 C.	1-2/3 C.	2 C.
Seasoned breadcrumbs	2/3 C.	1-1/3 C.	2 C.	2-2/3 C.	3-1/3 C.	4 C.
7 oz salmon fillets, skin removed	4	8	12	16	20	24

Assembly Directions:

Preheat oven to 375 degrees. Place vinegar, sugar and both mustards in small bowl and mix well. Whisk in oil until well blended. Spoon 1-2 tablespoons sauce over each fillet, covering completely. Press breadcrumbs onto fish. Bake salmon until cooked through, about 18 minutes.

Freezing Directions:

Cool completely. Transfer fillets to freezer wrap or foil, wrap tightly without mashing and place in rigid freezer container. Seal, label and freeze.

Serving Directions:

To thaw, unwrap frozen salmon and place in a single layer on a tray. Cover loosely with plastic wrap and leave in the refrigerator until completely thawed. To reheat, place the salmon on a microwave safe plate, heat on med-hi 2 minutes. Test the temperature and continue heating on high for 1 minute intervals until hot.

Nutritional Info: Baked Salmon with Mustard Crumb Crust

Per Serving: 491 Calories; 26g Fat (48.4% calories from fat); 43g Protein; 20g Carbohydrate; 1g Dietary Fiber; 104mg Cholesterol; 759mg Sodium.

Exchanges: 1 Grain (Starch); 5-1/2 Lean Meat; 4 Fat; 1/2 Other Carbohydrates.

Meatless Recipes

- Cheese-Filled Shells
- Quiche in a Bag
- Tex-Mex Lasagna
- Pasta with Herb Sauce
- Baked Ziti
- Spicy Tofu Enchiladas

Meatless Recipes

TIPS FOR MEATLESS RECIPES

General Tips for Meatless Recipes

■ Don't make the mistake of thinking that you can't eat meatless and be a freezer cook. Just follow the freezing tips and rules and apply them to the recipes that you already make. If your recipe depends upon using fresh vegetables, see if there are other parts of the recipe that could be made ahead of time and frozen. You can always add the veggies just before the final cooking time.

■ Eating meatless doesn't have to mean searching a vegetarian cookbook or trying "weirdo" foods. It can be as easy as replacing the meat in one of your favorite meals with tofu, legumes, nuts or vegetables.

■ Herbs will keep for several months in the freezer. Leaves from larger-leafed herbs like basil and sage should be removed from their stems, while tiny-leafed herbs like thyme and dill may be frozen while still on the stem. Wash and dry the herbs, then store individual varieties in sealed plastic bags or small freezer containers, labeled and dated. Frozen herbs often become limp or rubbery, so use them in dishes that call for some simmering, like soups or pasta sauces.

■ When freezing your food, divide it up into portion sizes first so that you do not need to thaw the entire quantity when you want some. Your food will stay fresher, and if you do this with several dishes, you will have a variety of items to choose from in your freezer for a quick meal. If you need more than one portion, simply take out more than one package.

■ In many recipes, you can create your own egg substitute by any of the following methods: use one ounce of mashed tofu; use 1/2 mashed banana in sweet recipes; mix one tablespoon of flax meal with two tablespoons water; or use one tablespoon of cornstarch or arrowroot mixed with two tablespoons of water. These techniques will help the recipe to "bind" when eggs are included for that purpose.

■ Rice freezes great! Fully cook it and when cooled, package it in various sized freezer bags. Remove all of the air and freeze the bags flat. Rice can be reheated on the stovetop or in the microwave and served with steamed vegetables, bean burritos, tacos, vegetarian chili, or used to fill cabbage rolls, make fried rice or rice pudding.

■ Freezing uncooked rice is fine too. Buy it in bulk and store it in the freezer safely for up to 2 years.

■ Tofu can be frozen up to 5 months. Defrosted tofu has a pleasant caramel color and a chewy, spongy texture that soaks up marinade sauces and is great for the grill. For freezing, buy firm or extra-firm tofu. (Silken tofu will turn mushy.) Remove the tofu from its packaging and drain the tofu slightly. Pat the tofu dry with a paper towel and cut it into desired shapes (this speeds the thawing process later). Wrap each piece individually in plastic wrap and then put all the wrapped pieces into a freezer bag. Press the excess air out of the freezer bag and seal the bag.

30 Day Gourmet Website Recipes & Tips

■ For more great 30 Day Gourmet meatless recipes, check out the recipes section of our website at: www.30daygourmet.com

■ For more meatless freezing tips and recipes from our cooks, check out the *Cooking-Meatless* section of our message boards at www.30daygourmet.com

■ Many freezer cooks find us because someone in their family has been diagnosed with a food intolerance and they are trying to find ways to cook "homemade" foods to accommodate that. Our message boards have a section for *Cooking-Special Diets* that you might find helpful. Lots of tips and great recipes for the freezer.

Recipe: Cheese-Filled Shells

Recipes:	1	2	3	4	5	6
Servings:	8	16	24	32	40	48
Makes: shells	40	80	120	160	200	240
Ingredients:						
Jumbo shells	40	80	120	160	200	240
Cottage cheese	32 oz.	64 oz.	96 oz.	128 oz.	160 oz.	192 oz.
Shredded mozzarella cheese	16 oz.	32 oz.	48 oz.	64 oz.	80 oz.	96 oz.
Grated parmesan cheese	3/4 C.	1-1/2 C.	2-1/4 C.	3 C.	3-3/4 C.	4-1/2 C.
Eggs	3	6	9	12	15	18
Oregano	3/4 t.	1-1/2 t.	2-1/4 t.	1 T.	1 T. + 3/4 t.	1 T. + 1-1/2 t.
Salt	1/2 t.	1 t.	1-1/2 t.	2 t.	2-1/2 t.	3 t.
Pepper	1/2 t.	1 t.	1-1/2 t.	2 t.	2-1/2 t.	3 t.
On Hand:						
*Spaghetti sauce	28 oz.	56 oz.	84 oz.	112 oz.	140 oz.	168 oz.

Assembly Directions:
Cook jumbo shells 1/2 of recommended time until just limp. Drain. Cool in a single layer on pan or waxed paper. Combine cheeses, eggs, oregano, salt and pepper. Fill each shell with 2 T. cheese mixture.

Tip: Using an icing bag with a wide tip works well for this or make your own by snipping the corner off a freezer bag.

Freezing Directions:
Freeze quantity of shells for one meal in a rigid container. Freeze sauce in freezer bag.

Serving Directions:
Thaw cheese-filled shells and sauce. Spread 1/2 C. spaghetti sauce in bottom of 9 x 13 baking dish. Arrange shells in dish. Pour remaining sauce over shells. Warm at 350 degrees for 30 minutes.

Comments:
Most kids really like these. They can be totally fat free depending on your cheese, sauce and egg choices. You could also use manicotti shells and whole wheat pasta works fine.

*See our Zippy Spaghetti Sauce recipe on page 55. You can leave out the meat if you want a meatless dish.

Nutritional Info: Cheese-Filled Shells
Nutritional info was calculated using meatless spaghetti sauce.

Per Serving: 667 Calories; 24g Fat (32.6% calories from fat); 43g Protein; 66g Carbohydrate; 4g Dietary Fiber; 136mg Cholesterol; 1440mg Sodium.

Exchanges: 3-1/2 Grain (Starch); 4-1/2 Lean Meat; 2-1/2 Fat.

Nutritional information for a "lite" version of this recipe may be found on page 139.

Recipe: Quiche in a Bag

Recipes:	1	2	3	4	5	6
Servings:	**6**	**12**	**18**	**24**	**30**	**36**
Ingredients:						
Cooked meat (any meat diced or browned and crumbled)	1 C.	2 C.	3 C.	4 C.	5 C.	6 C.
Vegetable (any *raw, blanched; thawed frozen; or canned, drained)	3/4 C.	1-1/2 C.	2-1/4 C.	3 C.	3-3/4 C.	4-1/2 C.
Shredded cheddar cheese	1 C.	2 C.	3 C.	4 C.	5 C.	6 C.
Diced onion	1/4 C.	1/2 C.	3/4 C.	1 C.	1-1/4 C.	1-1/2 C.
Milk	2 C.	4 C.	6 C.	8 C.	10 C.	12 C.
Eggs	4	8	12	16	20	24
Tabasco sauce	1/8 t.	1/4 t.	3/8 t.	1/2 t.	1/2 t. + 1/8 t.	3/4 t.
Flour	1/2 C.	1 C.	1-1/2 C.	2 C.	2-1/2 C.	3 C.
Baking powder	2 t.	1 T. + 1 t.	2 T.	2 T. + 2 t.	3 T. + 1 t.	4 T.

Assembly Directions:

Combine meat, vegetable, cheese and onion. Place this mixture in a labeled one-gallon freezer bag. With a mixer or blender, combine the milk, eggs, Tabasco sauce, flour and baking powder. Pour into the bag with the meat/vegetable mixture.

Freezing Directions:

Seal, label and freeze.

Serving Directions:

Thaw completely. Shake bag well and pour into spray-treated or greased deep-dish pie plate or quiche pan. Sprinkle with paprika if desired. Bake at 350 degrees for 30 to 45 minutes, until lightly browned on top and well set in the center. Cool about 5 minutes before serving.

Comments:

This is one of those dishes that you can get on the table when you haven't even looked in the freezer until 5:30 (like Nanci usually doesn't!). Just thaw the bag in the microwave, pour in a dish, and pop it in the oven. *For a vegetarian meal, just leave out the meat and increase the veggies by 1 C. for each recipe.
*See our Blanching Chart on page 133 if you are using fresh vegetables.

Nutritional Info: Quiche in a Bag

Calculated using sausage for the meat.
Per Serving: 369 Calories; 27g Fat (66.1% calories from fat); 17g Protein; 14g Carbohydrate; trace Dietary Fiber; 178mg Cholesterol; 626mg Sodium.
Exchanges: 1/2 Grain (Starch); 1 Lean Meat; 1/2 Non-Fat Milk; 1-1/2 Fat.

Nutritional Info: Quiche in a Bag - Lite

Replace sausage with extra lean ham, cheddar cheese with low fat cheddar cheese and 2% milk with skim milk.
Per Serving: 174 Calories; 6g Fat (29.4% calories from fat); 16g Protein; 14g Carbohydrate; trace Dietary Fiber; 140mg Cholesterol; 590mg Sodium.
Exchanges: 1/2 Grain (Starch); 1-1/2 Lean Meat; 1/2 Non-Fat Milk; 1/2 Fat.

Recipe: Tex-Mex Lasagna

Recipes:	1	2	3	4	5	6
Servings:	6	12	18	24	30	36
Makes: 9 x 13 pan	1	2	3	4	5	6
Ingredients:						
Spaghetti sauce; meatless	3 C.	6 C.	9 C.	12 C.	15 C.	18 C.
Water	1 C.	2 C	3 C.	4 C.	5 C.	6 C.
Kidney beans; canned, drained	15 oz.	30 oz.	45 oz.	60 oz.	75 oz.	90 oz.
Frozen corn	10 oz.	20 oz.	30 oz.	40 oz.	50 oz.	60 oz.
Chili seasoning mix envelope	1	2	3	4	5	6
Lasagna noodles	12	24	36	48	60	72
Part skim ricotta cheese	2 C.	4 C.	6 C.	8 C.	10 C.	12 C.
Monterey Jack Cheese, shredded	1-1/2 C.	3 C.	4-1/2 C.	6 C.	7-1/2 C.	9 C.

Assembly Directions:

Combine spaghetti sauce, water, beans, corn, and chili seasoning mix. Spread 1 cup of the combined sauce over the bottom of a 9x13 pan. Arrange 4 uncooked lasagna noodles over the sauce layer (3 lengthwise and one cross-wise). Cover the noodles with 1 cup of the combined sauce. Spread half of the ricotta over the sauce layer. Arrange another 4 pieces of the lasagna over the ricotta layer and top with one cup of combined sauce. Spread remaining ricotta over the top. Arrange the final 4 pieces of lasagna over the ricotta. Cover the casserole with all remaining combined sauce.

Freezing Directions:

Place the shredded cheese in a small plastic bag that can be taped or otherwise attached to the dish.
Wrap pan tightly with freezer paper, foil or place dish in a 2-gallon bag. Seal, label and freeze.

Serving Directions:

Thaw. Bake covered at 350 degrees for 45 minutes. Uncover lasagna, sprinkle the cheese on and bake uncovered for 15 minutes more.

Comments:

Lasagna will set up better and slice neater if it is allowed to sit for ten minutes before cutting.

Nutritional Info: Tex-Mex Lasagna

Per Serving: 528 Calories; 13g Fat (21.4% calories from fat); 22g Protein; 81g Carbohydrate; 6g Dietary Fiber; 33mg Cholesterol; 500mg Sodium.
Exchanges: 5-1/2 Grain (Starch); 1 Lean Meat; 1-1/2 Fat.

Nutritional information for a "lite" version of this recipe may be found on page 139.

Recipe: Pasta with Herb Sauce

Recipes:	1	2	3	4	5	6
Servings:	6	12	18	24	30	36
Sauce Ingredients:						
Milk	1/4 C.	1/2 C.	3/4 C.	1 C.	1-1/4 C.	1-1/2 C.
Grated parmesan cheese	1/4 C.	1/2 C.	3/4 C.	1 C.	1-1/4 C.	1-1/2 C.
Ricotta cheese	1/4 C.	1/2 C.	3/4 C.	1 C.	1-1/4 C.	1-1/2 C.
Green onions, sliced	2	4	6	8	10	12
Dried basil leaves	2 t.	1 T. + 1 t.	2 T.	2 T. + 2 t.	3 T. + 1 t.	4 T.
Minced garlic	1/2 t.	1 t.	1-1/2 t.	2 t.	2-1/2 t.	3 t.
Salt	1/2 t.	1 t.	1-1/2 t.	2 t.	2-1/2 t.	3 t.
Pasta Ingredients:						
Water	2 qts.	4 qts.	6 qts.	8 qts.	10 qts.	12 qts.
Fettuccini or any pasta	6 oz.	12 oz.	18 oz.	24 oz.	30 oz.	36 oz.

Assembly Directions:
Sauce: Puree the sauce ingredients together in a blender or food processor.
Pasta: Bring water to a boil. Add the salt and pasta. Bring back to a boil, and then reduce the heat until it is gently bubbling and will not boil over. Cook pasta for a total of 8 minutes then drain it well.
To serve without freezing, fully cook and drain the pasta, then toss the pasta with the sauce. Serve with grated Parmesan cheese.

Freezing Directions:
Freeze cooled, drained pasta in a freezer bag or rigid freezer container. Place sauce in a separate smaller container or bag. Attach to the pasta, or place both components in a larger freezer bag. Seal, label and freeze.

Serving Directions:
Thaw pasta and sauce thoroughly. Bring a 2-quart pot of water to boil. Drop pasta into boiling water and cook to desired tenderness (about 5 minutes) Drain and stir in thawed sauce. Serve immediately, or too much of the sauce will soak into the pasta. Pass additional Parmesan cheese at the table.

Comments:
Freshly boiled or steamed vegetables are very good stirred into the pasta. Try adding up to 4 C. of your favorite vegetables per recipe. Sliced carrots, broccoli florets, summer squash or snow peas per work well.

Nutritional Info: Pasta with Herb Sauce
Per Serving: 145 Calories; 3g Fat (18.7% calories from fat); 7g Protein; 23g Carbohydrate; 1g Dietary Fiber; 9mg Cholesterol; 266mg Sodium.
Exchanges: 1-1/2 Grain (Starch); 1/2 Lean Meat; 1/2 Fat.

Nutritional information for a "lite" version of this recipe may be found on page 139.

Recipe: Baked Ziti

Recipes:	1	2	3	4	5	6
Servings:	6	12	18	24	30	36
Ingredients:						
Eggs	1	2	3	4	5	6
Cottage Cheese OR Ricotta Cheese	2 C. or 12 oz.	4 C. or 24 oz.	6 C. or 36 oz.	8 C. or 48 oz.	10 C. or 60 oz.	12 C. or 72 oz.
Ziti pasta, slightly undercooked	16 oz.	32 oz.	48 oz.	64 oz.	80 oz.	96 oz.
Spaghetti sauce	1-1/2 C.	3 C.	4-1/2 C.	6 C.	7-1/2 C.	9 C.
Spinach; frozen, cooked and well drained	10 oz.	20 oz.	30 oz.	40 oz.	50 oz.	60 oz.

Assembly Directions:
In a food processor, combine the egg and cottage (or ricotta) cheese, and then mix all the ingredients together in a bowl.

Freezing Directions:
Place the entire mixture into freezer containers or freezer bags. Remove all the excess air. Seal, label and freeze.

Serving Directions:
Thaw the ziti mixture and bake in a sprayed 2-1/2 or 3 quart casserole. Bake at 350 degrees for 30 minutes. Additional cheese may be added to the top of the casserole before baking, if desired. Serve with Parmesan cheese.

Nutritional Info: Baked Ziti - Cottage Cheese
Meatless spaghetti sauce used for the nutritional analysis.
Per Serving: 406 Calories; 5g Fat (10.8% calories from fat); 23g Protein; 66g Carbohydrate; 4g Dietary Fiber; 37mg Cholesterol; 613mg Sodium.
Exchanges: 4 Grain (Starch); 1-1/2 Lean Meat; 1/2 Vegetable; 1/2 Fat.

Nutritional Info: Baked Ziti - Cottage Cheese Lite
Meatless spaghetti sauce used for nutritional analysis. Replace cottage cheese with low fat cottage cheese.
Per Serving: 393 Calories; 4g Fat (9.6% calories from fat); 22g Protein; 66g Carbohydrate; 4g Dietary Fiber; 34mg Cholesterol; 613mg Sodium.
Exchanges: 4 Grain (Starch); 1-1/2 Lean Meat; 1/2 Vegetable; 1/2 Fat.

Nutritional Info: Baked Ziti - Ricotta Cheese
Meatless spaghetti sauce used for nutritional analysis.
Per Serving: 437 Calories; 11g Fat (22.2% calories from fat); 19g Protein; 65g Carbohydrate; 4g Dietary Fiber; 60mg Cholesterol; 355mg Sodium.
Exchanges: 4 Grain (Starch); 1 Lean Meat; 1/2 Vegetable; 1 Fat.

Nutritional Info: Baked Ziti - Ricotta Cheese Lite
Meatless spaghetti sauce used for nutritional analysis. Replaced ricotta cheese with low fat ricotta cheese.
Per Serving: 393 Calories; 6g Fat (13.8% calories from fat); 19g Protein; 66g Carbohydrate; 4g Dietary Fiber; 49mg Cholesterol; 444mg Sodium.
Exchanges: 4 Grain (Starch); 1 Lean Meat; 1/2 Vegetable; 1/2 Fat.

Recipe: Spicy Tofu Enchiladas

Recipes:	1	2	3	4	5	6
Servings:	6	12	18	24	30	36
Makes:	12	24	36	48	60	72
Ingredients:						
Kidney beans; canned, drained and divided	15 oz.	30 oz.	45 oz.	60 oz.	75 oz.	90 oz.
Salsa (as spicy as you like it)	1 C.	2 C.	3 C.	4 C.	5 C.	6 C.
Salt	1/2 t.	1 t.	1-1/2 t.	2 t.	2-1/2 t.	3 t.
Onion powder	1/4 t.	1/2 t.	3/4 t.	1 t.	1-1/4 t.	1-1/2 t.
Diced onion	1/2 C.	1 C.	1-1/2 C.	2 C.	2-1/2 C.	3 C.
Minced garlic	1/2 t.	1 t.	1-1/2 t.	2 t.	2-1/2 t.	3 t.
Firm tofu, crumbled	1 lb.	2 lbs.	3 lbs.	4 lbs.	5 lbs.	6 lbs.
Cumin	1/2 t.	1 t.	1-1/2 t.	2 t.	2-1/2 t.	3 t.
Chili powder	1 t.	2 t.	1 T.	1 T. + 1 t.	1 T. + 2 t.	2 T.
6 inch corn tortillas	12	24	36	48	60	72
Shredded cheddar cheese	1 C.	2 C.	3 C.	4 C.	5 C.	6 C.
On Hand:						
Enchilada sauce	15 oz.	30 oz.	45 oz.	60 oz.	75 oz.	90 oz.

Assembly Directions:

Place one half of the kidney beans in a bowl and smash them with a fork. Add the salsa and stir until well blended. Add the remaining kidney beans, salt and onion powder. Spray skillet with cooking spray. Place onion, garlic, tofu, cumin and chili powder in skillet and sauté until tofu is lightly browned and onions are translucent. Pour salsa/bean mixture in skillet and cook until mixture is heated through and slightly thickened. This should take 5 to 10 minutes.

Freezing Directions:

Allow mixture to cool. Warm the corn tortillas in microwave to soften them. Place 2 or 3 tablespoons of mixture in the middle of the tortilla and roll up burrito style. Place on a baking sheet. Do this for all of the remaining tortillas. Flash freeze the enchiladas. When enchiladas are frozen, place in a gallon freezer bag or a rigid freezer container. Place the cheese in a separate freezer bag or snack bag and place inside the container of enchiladas. Seal, label and freeze.

Serving Directions:

Thaw enchiladas and cheese in the refrigerator. Spray a 9 x 13 pan with cooking spray and place enchiladas in the pan. Pour enchilada sauce over the top. Sprinkle cheese over the enchilada sauce. Bake at 350 degrees for 20 to 30 minutes or until the cheese is melted and sauce begins to bubble.

Nutritional Info: Spicy Tofu Enchiladas

Per Serving: 424 Calories; 20g Fat (40% calories from fat); 19g Protein; 47g Carbohydrate; 10g Dietary Fiber; 43mg Cholesterol; 829mg Sodium.

Exchanges: 3 Grain (Starch); 2-1/2 Lean Meat; 1-1/2 Vegetable; 3 Fat.

Nutritional information for a "lite" version of this recipe may be found on page 139.

Breads & Breakfast Recipes

- Tara's Favorite Muffins
- Apple Bread
- Super-Easy Freezer Cresent Rolls
- Breakfast McBiscuits
- Bread Machine Mix
- Breakfast Casserole

Breads & Breakfast Recipes

TIPS FOR BREADS & BREAKFAST RECIPES

General Tips for Breads & Breakfasts

- Breads (quick or bread machine) have 12 servings per loaf.
- One McBiscuit or muffin is considered a serving. Two crescent rolls are a serving.
- When I was a kid (a long time ago) we ate out once a month (always on a Friday night) when we shopped at the Pontiac Mall. By the time I was in high school, the fast food restaurants began to lure us in for lunch. Who would have ever thought that there would come a day when people would think nothing of eating breakfast on the run? So many breakfast foods can easily be made ahead of time and packed individually in the freezer. The money you will save really adds up! Muffins, Egg Casseroles, Quick Breads, and even homemade "McBiscuits" are a cinch to make ahead!
- Single-sized freezer packaging can be a key in getting your family to eat breakfast foods from the freezer. Make it as easy as possible for them to take out a serving, pop it in the microwave or toaster oven and go, go, go!
- Waffles and pancakes can be made ahead of time and frozen. Be sure to cool them before freezing. Separate them in small food storage bags (put inside a large freezer bag) so they don't stick together or stack them in a rigid freezer container with layers of plastic wrap or wax paper between each waffle/pancake. Reheat in the toaster (waffles) or microwave (pancakes and waffles).
- It's also easy to freeze homemade bread. Frozen bread keeps and freshens well. To freeze, allow the loaf to cool before placing it in freezer bags. Remove all of the air from the bag or ice crystals will form during the freezing process. Allow bread to thaw inside plastic bags to re-absorb the moisture lost during the freezing process. To freshen, place on a baking sheet and heat 10 to 15 minutes at 350 degrees.

- To successfully freeze muffins and quick breads, bake them completely, turn them out immediately, and then cool them thoroughly! Place the completely cooled muffins on a tray or baking sheet and open freeze them (no covering) for about a half hour or until they are firm to the touch. Place the frozen muffins into freezer bags or rigid freezer containers, remove any excess air, seal the container and store them in the freezer.

Healthy Tips for Breads and Breakfast

- The "Lite" recipes for our nutritional information substitute skim milk for 2%, reduced fat sour cream for regular sour cream, reduced fat cheese/cottage cheese for regular cheese/cottage cheese, light cream cheese for regular cream cheese, reduced fat mayonnaise for regular mayonnaise, and turkey bacon for bacon.
- When you freezer cook, it's easy to "sneak" healthy ingredients in on your family. Because you are working with lots of foods all at one time, they are less likely to notice the whole-wheat flour or the soy milk sitting out on the counter. Experiment with substitutions that will boost the nutritional value of your foods.
- Consider spending a few minutes and making up your own flavored oatmeal packets. You will save lots of money and they will be healthier than the pre-packaged versions. Freeze them in snack size freezer bags. Recipe with variations can be found on our message boards in the *Cooking-Breads & Breakfast* section.

30 Day Gourmet Website Recipes & Tips

- For more great 30 Day Gourmet breads and breakfast recipes, check out the recipes section of our website at: www.30daygourmet.com
- For more breads and breakfast freezing tips and recipes from our cooks, check out the *Cooking-Breads & Breakfast* section of our message boards at www.30daygourmet.com

Recipe: Tara's Favorite Muffins

Recipes:	1	2	3	4	5	6
Servings:	12	24	36	48	60	72
Makes: muffins	12	24	36	48	60	72
Ingredients:						
Eggs	2	4	6	8	10	12
Sugar	1 C.	2 C.	3 C.	4 C.	5 C.	6 C.
Vegetable Oil	1/2 C.	1 C.	1-1/2 C.	2 C.	2-1/2 C.	3 C.
Vanilla	1 t.	2 t.	1 T.	1 T. + 1 t.	1 T. + 2 t.	2 T.
Salt	1/2 t.	1 t.	1-1/2 t.	2 t.	2-1/2 t.	1 T.
Sour Cream	8 oz.	16 oz.	24 oz.	32 oz.	40 oz.	48 oz.
Flour	2 C.	4 C.	6 C.	8 C.	10 C.	12 C.
Baking soda	1/2 t.	1 t.	1-1/2 t.	2 t.	2-1/2 t.	1 T.
Baking powder	1 t.	2 t.	1 T.	1 T. + 1 t.	1 T. + 2 t.	2 T.

Assembly Directions:

In a large bowl, beat eggs. Add sugar, oil, vanilla, salt, and sour cream, mixing well. All at one time, add flour, baking soda and baking powder. Stir until all is moistened and slightly lumpy. Pour into oiled muffin cups filled 2/3 full and bake at 400 degrees for 20 minutes. These full size muffins freeze and thaw very well.

Freezing Directions:

Allow to cool. Place muffins in freezer bags or rigid containers. Seal, label and freeze.

Serving Directions:

Thaw in refrigerator or at room temperature. They can be warmed in the microwave after thawing. Microwave on high for 10 to 15 seconds.

Comments:

1 cup of blueberries, nuts, or raisins may be added.
For spice muffins, with the flour, add 1/2 t. cinnamon, 1/4 t. ground nutmeg, 1/8 t. ground cloves.
To give interesting texture to plain muffins, substitute 1/4 cup of cornmeal for 1/4 cup of the flour.

Nutritional Info: Tara's Favorite Muffins

Per Serving: 273 Calories; 14g Fat (45.8% calories from fat); 4g Protein; 34g Carbohydrate; 1g Dietary Fiber; 40mg Cholesterol; 202mg Sodium.
Exchanges: 1 Grain (Starch); 2-1/2 Fat; 1 Other Carbohydrates.

Nutritional Info: Tara's Favorite Muffins - Lite

Replace sour cream with light sour cream and half of the oil with unsweetened applesauce.
Per Serving: 201 Calories; 6g Fat (25.9% calories from fat); 3g Protein; 34g Carbohydrate; 1g Dietary Fiber; 33mg Cholesterol; 197mg Sodium.
Exchanges: 1 Grain (Starch); 1 Fat; 1 Other Carbohydrates.

Nutritional information for muffin variations is available in the Members' section of our website at www.30daygourmet.com

Recipe: Apple Bread

Recipes:	1	2	3	4	5	6
Servings:	12	24	36	48	60	72
Makes: loaves	1	2	3	4	5	6
Ingredients:						
Margarine	1/2 C.	1 C.	1-1/2 C.	2 C.	2-1/2 C.	3 C.
Eggs	2	4	6	8	10	12
Sugar	1 C.	2 C.	3 C.	4 C.	5 C.	6 C.
Baking soda	1 t.	2 t.	1 T.	1 T. + 1 t.	1 T. + 2 t.	2 T.
Salt	1/2 t.	1 t.	1-1/2 t.	2 t.	2-1/2 t.	1 T.
Vanilla	1 t.	2 t.	1 T.	1 T. + 1 t.	1 T. + 2 t.	2 T.
Flour	2 C.	4 C.	6 C.	8 C.	10 C.	12 C.
Sliced apples	2 C.	4 C.	6 C.	8 C.	10 C.	12 C.
Chopped nuts (optional)	1/2 C.	1 C.	1-1/2 C.	2 C.	2-1/2 C.	3 C.
Topping:						
Margarine (very soft)	2 T.	1/4 C.	1/4 C. + 2T.	1/2 C.	1/2 C. + 2T.	3/4 C.
Flour	3 T.	1/4 C. + 2T.	1/2 C. + 1T.	3/4 C.	3/4 C. + 3T.	1 C. + 2 T.
Brown sugar	3 T.	1/4 C. + 2T.	1/2 C. + 1T.	3/4 C.	3/4 C. + 3T.	1 C. + 2 T.
Cinnamon	1 T.	2 T.	3 T.	1/4 C.	1/4 C. + 1T.	1/4 C. + 2T.

Assembly Directions:
Blend margarine, eggs and sugar together. Add soda, salt and vanilla; beat. Add flour, mix, and then add apples and nuts. Place in greased bread pan. Mix topping ingredients together until crumbly. Sprinkle on top of breads. Bake at 325 degrees for 55-60 minutes.

Freezing Directions:
Wrap in plastic wrap, then in aluminum foil. Seal, label and freeze.

Serving Directions:
Allow the bread to thaw. Slice and enjoy.

Comments:
It's really good warmed up in the microwave with a little bit of butter on it!

Nutritional Info: Apple Bread
Per Serving: 303 Calories; 14g Fat (40.8% calories from fat); 5g Protein; 41g Carbohydrate; 2g Dietary Fiber; 36mg Cholesterol; 318mg Sodium.
Exchanges: 1-1/2 Grain (Starch); 2-1/2 Fat; 1-1/2 Other Carbohydrates.

Recipe: Super-Easy Freezer Crescent Rolls

Recipes:	1	2	3	4	5	6
Servings:	24	48	72	96	120	144
Makes: rolls	48	96	144	192	240	288
Ingredients:						
Milk, scalded	2 C.	4 C.	6 C.	8 C.	10 C.	12 C.
Butter or margarine	1/2 C.	1 C.	1-1/12 C.	2 C.	2-1/2 C.	3 C.
Flour, sifted; divided	7 C.	14 C.	21 C.	28 C.	35 C.	42 C.
Yeast; not Quick Rise	2 env.	4 env.	6 env.	8 env.	10 env.	12 env.
Sugar	1/2 C.	1 C.	1-1/2 C.	2 C.	2-1/2 C.	3 C.
Salt	2 t.	1 T. + 1 t.	2 T.	2 T. + 2 t.	3 T. + 1 t.	1/4 C.
Eggs, slightly beaten	2	4	6	8	10	12

Assembly Directions:

To scald the milk, put it in a saucepan over medium heat. Watch it, and when small bubbles start to form around the edges, it's done. It doesn't boil and the bottom doesn't scorch. Remove from heat and add the butter, so it melts in the warm milk. Set aside to cool slightly. In a large bowl, mix together 4 C. of flour, yeast, sugar and salt. Check the temperature of the milk… it needs to be between 120 to 130 degrees F to activate the yeast. When the milk is the right temperature, mix it to the flour mixture. Mix in the eggs and the remaining 3 C. of flour. Make sure the dough is well mixed, but do not knead. The dough will be sticky. Cover and let rise for 2 hours in a warm, draft-free place. After 2 hours, punch the dough down, and let it rest for 5 minutes. Divide the dough into 6 equal pieces. Lightly dust the counter with flour, and roll one piece into a circle as large as you can get it. It doesn't have to be a perfect circle! Dip your hand, a spreader or a spatula into the tub of margarine and spread a thin layer all over the circle. Next, cut the circle into 8 pie-shaped pieces with a pizza cutter. This doesn't have to be perfect either… mine come out all sizes! Using your hands, roll up each pie-shaped piece, starting at the wide end and rolling towards the small end. Place it seam-side down on a cookie sheet. Repeat this process until all the dough is used up.

Freezing Directions:

Place the cookie sheet(s) of dough rolls into the freezer. When they're frozen solid, place them in a container with a lid or a freezer bag. Seal, label and freeze. Keep in the freezer until ready to use. (They don't seem to rise well if you keep them longer than 3 months.)

Serving Directions:

Grease a cookie sheet and place the needed number of frozen rolls on it. Cover and let rise in a warm, draft-free place for 3-1/2 to 4 hours, or until doubled. (When dough is doubled, you can touch it with your finger and the indentation will stay.) Preheat your oven to 350 degrees, and bake the rolls for 10-15 minutes, or until lightly browned. Brush lightly with melted butter and serve.

Comments:

This is the best and easiest recipe I have ever found for frozen dinner rolls! Best of all, it required NO kneading! They turn out great every time.

Nutritional Info: Super-Easy Freezer Crescent Rolls

Per Serving: 217 Calories; 7g Fat (28.5% calories from fat); 5g Protein; 33g Carbohydrate; 1g Dietary Fiber; 17mg Cholesterol; 260mg Sodium.
Exchanges: 2 Grain (Starch); 1 Fat; 1/2 Other Carbohydrates.

Nutritional information for crescent roll tips and variations may be found in the Members' section of our website at
www.30daygourmet.com

Recipe: Breakfast McBiscuits

Recipes:	1	2	3	4	5	6
Servings:	12	24	36	48	60	72
Ingredients:						
Grands biscuits, baked	12	24	36	48	60	72
Pre-cooked bacon slices Or Ham slices Or Cooked sausage patties	24 or 12 or 12	48 or 24 or 24	72 or 36 or 36	96 or 48 or 48	120 or 60 or 60	144 or 72 or 72
Eggs; scrambled, fried or poached	1 dz.	2 dz.	3 dz.	4 dz.	5 dz.	6 dz.
Cheese slices	12	24	36	48	60	72

Assembly Directions:
Split baked biscuits. Top with your choice of topping combinations.
Example:
  2 slices of bacon, 1 egg, 1 slice of cheese OR
  1 sausage patty, 1 slice of cheese OR
  1/4 C. scrambled eggs, 1 slice of cheese
Be creative!

Freezing Directions:
Wrap individually, label, and freeze.

Serving Directions:
To serve, place thawed, foil-wrapped biscuit in oven and warm at 400 degrees for 20 minutes or unwrap and re-wrap in damp paper towel and microwave a few minutes.

Nutritional Info: Breakfast McBiscuits
Used Pillsbury Grands biscuits, bacon, egg and cheese slice in the calculations.
Per Serving: 443 Calories; 29g Fat (59.6% calories from fat); 20g Protein; 24g Carbohydrate; 1g Dietary Fiber; 227mg Cholesterol; 983mg Sodium.
Exchanges: 1-1/2 Grain (Starch); 2-1/2 Lean Meat; 4-1/2 Fat.

Nutritional Info: Breakfast McBiscuits - Lite
Replace regular Grands with reduced fat Grands, bacon with turkey bacon and cheddar cheese with low fat cheddar cheese.
Per Serving: 354 Calories; 19g Fat (47.5% calories from fat); 18g Protein; 29g Carbohydrate; 1g Dietary Fiber; 222mg Cholesterol; 1314mg Sodium.
Exchanges: 1-1/2 Grain (Starch); 2 Lean Meat; 2-1/2 Fat.

Recipe: Bread Machine Mix

Recipes:	1	2	3	4	5	6
Servings:	72	144	216	288	360	432
Makes:	21 C.	42 C.	63 C.	84 C.	105 C.	126 C.
Ingredients:						
All-purpose flour	5 lb. + 1 C.	10 lb. + 2 C.	15 lb. + 3 C.	20 lb. + 4 C.	25 lb. + 5 C.	30 lb. + 6 C.
Sugar or brown sugar	1 C.	2 C.	3 C.	4 C.	5 C.	6 C.
*Powdered buttermilk	1 C.	2 C.	3 C.	4 C.	5 C.	6 C.
Salt	1 t.	2 t.	1 T.	1 T. + 1 t.	1 T. + 2 t.	2 T.

Assembly Directions:
In a large bowl, mix together the flour, sugar, powdered buttermilk and salt. Mix well.

Freezing Directions:
Measure out 3-1/2 C. of the mixture into quart-size zipper bags. Each batch of the mix will yield 6 bags of mix. If you have a few tablespoons of mix left over after measuring out the 6 bags, just divide it between the bags. Put the bags of mix in a 2-gallon freezer bag, or into two 1-gallon freezer bags. Seal, label and freeze. Or, put the entire mix in an airtight rigid container, and store the whole thing in the freezer.

Serving Directions:
Remove a quart-size bag of the mixture from the freezer. Allow it to come to room temperature. Or, remove the large container of mix from the freezer. Measure out 3 1/2 C. of the mixture, and allow it to come to room temperature.   Place the following ingredients in your bread machine in the order recommended by the manufacturer:

1 C. warm water

1 egg

2 T. butter or cooking oil

3 1/2 C. bread mix

1 1/2 t. active dry yeast

Set your bread machine to the appropriate setting and press start. Makes a 1-1/2 pound loaf.

Comments:
This is a very versatile dough that can be used for cinnamon buns, pizza crust, hot pockets, and calzones in addition to bread. *Powdered Buttermilk can be found at your local grocery, probably in the baking aisle. They promote it to be used for baking, in place of liquid buttermilk. It has a longer refrigerator-life than liquid buttermilk.

Nutritional Info: Bread Machine Mix
Per Serving: 139 Calories; trace Fat (2.8% calories from fat); 4g Protein; 29g Carbohydrate; 1g Dietary Fiber; 1mg Cholesterol; 40mg Sodium.
Exchanges: 1-1/2 Grain (Starch).

Nutritional Info: Basic Bread Machine Bread
Per Serving: 163 Calories; 3g Fat (15.2% calories from fat); 5g Protein; 29g Carbohydrate; 1g Dietary Fiber; 17mg Cholesterol; 67mg Sodium.
Exchanges: 1-1/2 Grain (Starch); 1/2 Fat.

Recipe: Breakfast Egg Casserole

Recipes:	1	2	3	4	5	6
Servings:	6	12	18	24	30	36
Ingredients:						
Bread slices, crust removed if desired, make 1" cubes	8	16	24	32	40	48
Ham, diced	4 oz.	8 oz.	12 oz.	16 oz.	20 oz.	24 oz.
Shredded Swiss Cheese	4 oz.	8 oz.	12 oz.	16 oz.	20 oz.	24 oz.
Shredded Cheddar Cheese	4 oz.	8 oz.	12 oz.	16 oz.	20 oz.	24 oz.
Eggs	3	6	9	12	15	18
Milk	1 C.	2 C.	3 C.	4 C.	5 C.	6 C.
Onion powder	1/4 t.	1/2 t.	3/4 t.	1 t.	1-1/4 t.	1-1/2 t.
Salt	1/2 t.	1 t.	1-1/2 t.	2 t.	2-1/2 t.	1 T.
Dry mustard	1/2 t.	1 t.	1-1/2 t.	2 t.	2-1/2 t.	1 T.

Assembly Directions:

Place 1/2 the bread cubes in a greased 9" square or round baking pan, or other heatproof baking dish. Over the bread cubes, layer half of the diced ham and half of each shredded cheese. Repeat all the layers ending with a layer of cheese. The pan will be very full. Beat the remaining ingredients together and pour over the pan. Cover the pan loosely with plastic wrap and refrigerate overnight if serving the next day. If not, continue with freezing instructions.

Freezing Directions:

Cover the pan loosely with plastic wrap and place inside a labeled one-gallon freezer bag. Seal and freeze.

Serving Directions:

Thaw the pan in the refrigerator for about 12 to 14 hours. Remove from bag and discard plastic wrap. Bake in a 375 degree preheated oven for 35 – 40 minutes. Cool 5-10 minutes before slicing to serve.

Comments:

The doubled recipe will fill a 9x13" baking pan and serve 12 – 14. The casserole may be baked frozen. Bake it at 300 degrees for 25 minutes, then 350 degrees for 35 minutes. A half-pound of bacon or sausage, cooked, drained and crumbled may be substituted for the ham. A cup of sliced summer sausage, or similar sausage may also be substituted. A small can of drained shrimp or crab would also be good in this. A cup of cooked diced broccoli, fresh or canned mushrooms, or sweet bell pepper may be added.

Nutritional Info: Breakfast Egg Casserole

Ham was used in the nutritional analysis.
Per Serving: 324 Calories; 18g Fat (49.5% calories from fat); 20g Protein; 20g Carbohydrate; 1g Dietary Fiber; 145mg Cholesterol; 820mg Sodium.
Exchanges: 1 Grain (Starch); 2 Lean Meat; 2 Fat.

Nutritional information for a "lite" version of this recipe may be found on page 139.

Soup & Sandwich Recipes

- Beefy Vegetable Soup
- Cheddar Broccoli Soup
- Taco Chili
- Crock-pot Beef Sandwiches
- Pork Barbecue
- Crock-pot Hot Sausage Sandwiches

Soup & Sandwich Recipes

TIPS FOR SOUP & SANDWICH RECIPES

General Tips for Soups and Sandwiches

- 1 cup of soup or chili is considered a standard serving.
- 1/4 to 1/2 cup of barbecue or pulled beef is considered a standard serving.
- It's fine to freeze soups containing milk. When they are thawed, they may look curdled or separated, but once you heat them thru, they re-combine and are fine.
- You can freeze sandwiches of all kinds. Avoid soggy bread by using "day-old" and by not spreading mayonnaise on the bread before freezing. Butter and peanut butter work fine but mayo separates and soaks into the bread. Just wrap them individually in plastic wrap or sandwich bags and then put them into a rigid freezer container so that they don't get squished in the freezer.
- For PBJ's put peanut butter on both pieces of bread, with the jelly in the middle of the two and do not cut the sandwich until it is time to eat it. These things will prevent the bread from getting soggy.
- I ran into a 30 Day Gourmet in the parking lot at WalMart the other day. We spent our walk into the store (that can usually count for aerobics in our town) talking about her cooking day and how great it was. She shared a super idea for hot sandwiches with me. She and her daughter-in-law made up sloppy joe filling and had ham and cheese on hand. They bought buns and filled them with the sandwich fixin's. Then they wrapped them in the individual foil sheets and froze them. 20-30 minutes (wrapped) in the oven and you've got a great sandwich. No worry about whether you have buns on hand and it's easy to pull out just one or two. Thanks, Leslie!

Healthy Tips for Soups and Sandwiches

- The "Lite" recipes for our nutritional information substitute ground turkey for ground round, 2% milk with skim milk, regular cheese with low fat cheese and sour cream with light sour cream. Soups can be thickened in the same way that you would make fat free white sauce. This eliminates that need for some of the fat that is used in the regular white sauce.
- Homemade soup is so much healthier than the store brands. Make your own healthy substitutions. Low fat, low salt, low anything-you-like. Soups are also a great way to sneak some extra nutrition and fiber in on your family.

30 Day Gourmet Website Recipes & Tips

- For more great 30 Day Gourmet soups and sandwiches recipes, check out the recipes section of our website at: www.30daygourmet.com
- For more soups and sandwiches freezing tips and recipes from our cooks, check out the *Cooking-Soups & Sandwich* section of our message boards at www.30daygourmet.com

Nothing beats a bowl of homemade soup!

Recipe: Beefy Vegetable Soup

Recipes:	1	2	3	4	5	6
Servings:	8	16	24	32	40	48
Makes:	13 C.	26 C.	39 C.	52 C.	65 C.	78 C.
Ingredients:						
Chopped onion	1 C.	2 C.	3 C.	4 C.	5 C.	6 C.
Chopped celery	1 C.	2 C.	3 C.	4 C.	5 C.	6 C.
Tomatoes; canned, chopped, undrained	28 oz.	56 oz.	84 oz.	112 oz.	140 oz.	168 oz.
Ground beef, cooked and drained	5 C.	10 C.	15 C.	20 C.	25 C.	30 C.
Tomato sauce with tomato bits	15 oz.	30 oz.	45 oz.	60 oz.	75 oz.	90 oz.
Salt	2 t.	1 T. + 1 t.	2 T.	2 T. + 2 t.	3 T. + 1 t.	4 T.
Black pepper	1 t.	2 t.	1 T.	1 T. + 1 t.	1 T. + 2 t.	2 T.
On Hand:						
Butter or margarine	1/4 C.	1/2 C.	3/4 C.	1 C.	1-1/4 C.	1-1/2 C.
Flour	1/4 C.	1/2 C.	3/4 C.	1 C.	1-1/4 C.	1-1/2 C.
Beef broth	48 oz.	96 oz.	144 oz.	192 oz.	240 oz.	288 oz.
Mixed vegetables, frozen	10 oz.	20 oz.	30 oz.	40 oz.	50 oz.	60 oz.

Assembly Directions:
In a skillet, mix together the onion, celery, and canned chopped tomatoes and their liquid. Simmer until the celery and onion are tender. Stir in the cooked ground beef, tomato sauce, salt, and pepper. Set aside to cool.

Freezing Directions:
When cooled, place meat mixture in a labeled freezer container or bag. Seal, label, and freeze. Mark the top of broth can(s) with a permanent marker so that you will not use them accidentally. Also mark the frozen vegetables.

Serving Directions:
Thaw all frozen ingredients (beef/tomato mixture, and frozen vegetables). In a large pot, melt butter over medium low heat. Stir in flour and continue to cook and stir until a bubbly paste forms. Pour in beef broth and bring to a boil, stirring constantly. Add thawed vegetables and beef/tomato mixture. Return to a boil, then reduce heat and simmer until vegetables are tender.

Nutritional Info: Beefy Vegetable Soup
Per Serving: 416 Calories; 22g Fat (46.5% calories from fat); 35g Protein; 21g Carbohydrate; 4g Dietary Fiber; 79mg Cholesterol; 2049mg Sodium.
Exchanges: 4-1/2 Lean Meat;-2 1/2 Vegetable; 2 Fat.

Nutritional information for a "lite" version of this recipe may be found on page 139.

Recipe: Cheddar Broccoli Soup

Recipes:	1	2	3	4	5	6
Servings:	6	12	18	24	30	36
Ingredients:						
Frozen broccoli	20 oz.	40 oz.	60 oz.	80 oz.	100 oz.	120 oz.
OR	or	or	or	or	or	or
Fresh broccoli	1 bunch	2 bunches	3 bunches	4 bunches	5 bunches	6 bunches
Water	1 C.	2 C.	3 C.	4 C.	5 C.	6 C.
Finely chopped onion	1/4 C.	1/2 C.	3/4 C.	1 C.	1-1/4 C.	1-1/2 C.
Margarine or butter	1/3 C.	2/3 C.	1 C.	1-1/3 C.	1-2/3 C.	2 C.
Chicken bouillon granules	2 T.	1/4 C.	1/4 C. + 2 T.	1/2 C.	1/2 C. + 2 T.	3/4 C.
Hot water	1 C.	2 C.	3 C.	4 C.	5 C.	6 C.
Flour	1/2 C.	1 C.	1-1/2 C.	2 C.	2-1/2 C.	3 C.
Milk	2 C.	4 C.	6 C.	8 C.	10 C.	12 C.
Shredded cheddar cheese	2 C.	4 C.	6 C.	8 C.	10 C.	12 C.
Ground nutmeg	1/8 t.	1/4 t.	1/4 t. + 1/8 t.	1/2 t.	1/2 t. + 1/8 t.	3/4 t.

Assembly Directions:

If using fresh broccoli, cut it into chunks, including the stalk. Cook broccoli in water until tender. Don't drain. Pureé the broccoli and water in a food processor; set aside. (You should have about 2 C. puréed broccoli per batch.) Sauté onion in margarine until tender. Dissolve bouillon in hot water; set aside. Stir flour into butter/onion mixture. Gradually add the milk and water/bouillon, stirring constantly. Continue stirring until well blended and thick. Add the cheese, nutmeg and pureed broccoli. Cook until cheese melts and soup is hot. Don't boil the soup.

Freezing Directions:

Allow soup to cool completely. Package it for freezing based on how you want to serve it. If you will serve it all at once, freeze it in a 1 or 2-gallon freezer bag, or large rigid container. If you want single servings, freeze it in quart freezer bags or 2 C. rigid containers. Seal, label and freeze.

Serving Directions:

Thaw. Heat the soup in the microwave or on the stovetop until heated through. Do not boil. To keep warm for a gathering, keep the soup in a crock-pot on low.

Comments:

This recipe makes the best Cheddar Broccoli Soup. It makes a great lunch on a frosty winter day! If you like pieces of broccoli in your soup, you can save out 1/4 to 1/3 C. of small broccoli florets... don't puree them. Add them to the soup when you add the pureed broccoli.

Nutritional Info: Cheddar Broccoli Soup

Per Serving: 349 Calories; 25g Fat (62.2% calories from fat); 16g Protein; 18g Carbohydrate; 3g Dietary Fiber; 46mg Cholesterol; 450mg Sodium.

Exchanges: 1/2 Grain (Starch); 1-1/2 Lean Meat; 1 Vegetable; 1/2 Non-Fat Milk; 4 Fat.

Nutritional information for a "lite" version of this recipe may be found on page 139.

Recipe: Taco Chili

Recipes:	1	2	3	4	5	6
Servings:	12	24	36	48	60	72
Ingredients:						
Lean ground beef	2 lbs.	4 lbs.	6 lbs.	8 lbs.	10 lbs.	12 lbs.
Taco seasoning envelope	1	2	3	4	5	6
Crushed tomatoes, undrained	28 oz.	56 oz.	84 oz.	112 oz.	140 oz.	168 oz.
Salsa	15 oz.	30 oz.	45 oz.	60 oz.	75 oz.	90 oz.
Canned corn, undrained	15 oz.	30 oz.	45 oz.	60 oz.	75 oz.	90 oz.
Kidney beans, undrained	16 oz.	32 oz.	48 oz.	64 oz.	80 oz.	96 oz.
Black beans, drained and rinsed	15 oz.	30 oz.	45 oz.	60 oz.	75 oz.	90 oz.
On Hand:						
Sour cream	8 oz.	16 oz.	24 oz.	32 oz.	40 oz.	48 oz.
Shredded cheddar cheese	1 C.	2 C.	3 C.	4 C.	5 C.	6 C.
Tortilla chips for scooping	15 oz.	30 oz.	45 oz.	60 oz.	75 oz.	90 oz.

Assembly Directions:

Brown ground beef. Meanwhile, in a large bowl, combine the taco seasoning, tomatoes, salsa, corn, kidney beans and black beans. Stir to mix. When the ground beef is cooked, drain off any fat, then add it to the bowl of other ingredients and stir to combine.

Freezing Directions:

Freeze in freezer bags or rigid containers based on your family size. Seal, label and freeze.

Serving Directions:

Thaw overnight in the refrigerator. Heat mixture in a saucepan on the stove until it's hot and bubbly. Spoon into bowls. Top each bowl with a spoon of sour cream and a sprinkle of shredded cheddar cheese. Serve with tortilla chips on the side for scooping to eat it... don't use a spoon!

Comments:

You can control the spiciness by choosing mild or hot salsa. If you really like salsa, add a bigger jar. If you really like hot and spicy, add a 4-ounce can of diced green chilies, drained. You can add a can of sliced black olives (drained) too.

Nutritional Info: Taco Chili

Per Serving: 533 Calories; 27g Fat (45.7% calories from fat); 27g Protein; 46g Carbohydrate; 9g Dietary Fiber; 71mg Cholesterol; 1059mg Sodium.

Exchanges: 2 1/2 Grain (Starch); 3 Lean Meat; 1 Vegetable; 3-1/2 Fat.

Nutritional information for a "lite" version of this recipe may be found on page 139.

SOUP & SANDWICH RECIPES

Recipe: Crock-Pot Beef Sandwiches

Recipes:	1	2	3	4	5	6
Servings:	12	24	36	48	60	72
Makes:	4 C.	8 C.	12 C.	16 C.	20 C.	24 C.
Ingredients:						
Beef roast, chuck roast, or thick chuck steak, fat trimmed and discarded	2-1/2 lbs.	5 lbs.	7 1/2 lbs.	10 lbs.	12 1/2 lbs.	15 lbs.
Dry Italian or Ranch salad dressing packets OR Onion soup mix packets	2	4	6	8	10	12
Water	1 C.	2 C.	3 C.	4 C.	5 C.	6 C.
On Hand:						
Hamburger buns	12	24	36	48	60	72

Assembly Directions:

In a cold crock-pot, place the thawed or fresh roast. Pour the contents of the salad dressing or soup packets over the meat. Pour the water over all. Cover crock-pot with lid. Can be cooked overnight on low heat or 6 hours on high heat until meat shreds easily with a fork. When done, turn off crock-pot and uncover it to cool quickly. If you wish, the filling is now ready to eat. Follow the serving directions below.

Freezing Directions:

When cooled, place meat and juice in a freezer bag or container. Seal, label and freeze. (2 cups fills 8 average sized buns.)

Serving Directions:

Thaw and heat in a microwave or saucepan over medium heat until warmed through. Serve over rolls or in buns.

Comments:

Roasts over 7-1/ 2 lbs. may not fit well in a crock-pot. Try to borrow an extra crock-pot if you choose to make more than 7-1/ 2 lbs. This is a large recipe and we divide each recipe in half for freezing purposes. About 1/4-1/3 C of cooked meat is a serving. Barbecue Option: Reduce water by half. Pour water and 1 C. of barbecue sauce per recipe over all. (May add more barbecue sauce later to taste.)

Nutritional Info: Crock-Pot Beef Sandwiches - Italian
Per Serving: 327 Calories; 17g Fat (47.9% calories from fat); 19g Protein; 23g Carbohydrate; 1g Dietary Fiber; 55mg Cholesterol; 715mg Sodium. **Exchanges:** 1-1/2 Grain (Starch); 2 Lean Meat; 2 Fat.

Nutritional Info: Crock-Pot Beef Sandwiches - Ranch
Per Serving: 321 Calories; 17g Fat (48.6% calories from fat); 19g Protein; 22g Carbohydrate; 1g Dietary Fiber; 55mg Cholesterol; 310mg Sodium. **Exchanges:** 1-1/2 Grain (Starch); 2 Lean Meat; 2 Fat.

Nutritional Info: Crock-Pot Beef Sandwiches - BBQ
Reduce water by half. Replace onion soup mix with 1 cup of commercial barbecue sauce.
Per Serving: 336 Calories; 17g Fat (47.4% calories from fat); 19g Protein; 24g Carbohydrate; 1g Dietary Fiber; 55mg Cholesterol; 458mg Sodium. **Exchanges:** 1-1/2 Grain (Starch); 2 Lean Meat; 2 Fat.

SOUP & SANDWICH RECIPES

Recipe: Pork Barbecue

Recipes:	1	2	3	4	5	6
Servings:	6	12	18	24	30	36
Makes: sandwiches	6	12	18	24	30	36
Ingredients:						
Chopped onion	1/2 C.	1 C.	1-1/2 C.	2 C.	2-1/2 C.	3 C.
Chopped celery	1/2 C.	1 C.	1-1/2 C.	2 C.	2-1/2 C.	3 C.
Ketchup	1/2 C.	1 C.	1-1/2 C.	2 C.	2-1/2 C.	3 C.
Water	1/3 C.	2/3 C.	1 C.	1-1/3 C.	1-2/3 C.	2 C.
Lemon juice	2 T.	1/4 C.	1/4 C. + 2 T.	1/2 C.	1/2 C. + 2 T.	3/4 C.
Brown sugar or molasses	1 T.	2 T.	3 T.	1/4 C.	1/4 C. + 1 T.	1/4 C. + 2 T.
Worcestershire sauce	1 T.	2 T.	3 T.	1/4 C.	1/4 C. + 1 T.	1/4 C. + 2 T.
Vinegar	1 T.	2 T.	3 T.	1/4 C.	1/4 C. + 1 T.	1/4 C. + 2 T.
Prepared mustard	1 T.	2 T.	3 T.	1/4 C.	1/4 C. + 1 T.	1/4 C. + 2 T.
Salt and pepper to taste						
Pork Roast	1-1/2 lb.	3 lbs.	4-1/2 lbs.	6 lbs.	7-1/2 lbs.	9 lbs.
On Hand:						
Hoagie rolls or sandwich buns	6	12	18	24	30	36

Assembly Directions:

In slow cooker, stir all ingredients together except for meat. Set the meat on top of the sauce and simmer until meat is easily shredded with a fork. Simmer 6 to 8 hours over night. Shred meat while it is warm. Stir in the sauce well. The barbecued pork is now ready to eat, or cool for freezing.

Freezing Directions:

When the meat is cool, portion it into freezer bags or rigid containers. Seal, label and freeze.

Serving Directions:

Thaw the meat. Heat the meat in the microwave, in a saucepan on low, or in the oven at 350 degrees until hot (15 to 20 minutes per recipe).

Comments:

Options: Add a few drops of liquid smoke for a smoky flavor.
Diced bell peppers may be added to the sauce ingredients: 1/2 to 1 C. per recipe.

Nutritional Info: Pork Barbecue

Per Serving: 406 Calories; 13g Fat (29.7% calories from fat); 25g Protein; 46g Carbohydrate; 3g Dietary Fiber; 56mg Cholesterol; 729mg Sodium.
Exchanges: 2-1/2 Grain (Starch); 2-1/2 Lean Meat; 1 Fat; 1/2 Other Carbohydrates.

Recipe: Crock-Pot Hot Sausage Sandwiches

Recipes:	1	2	3	4	5	6
Servings:	9	18	27	36	45	54
Makes:	12 C.	24 C.	36 C.	48 C.	60 C.	72 C.
Ingredients:						
Onion, cut in large chunks	1 C.	2 C.	3 C.	4 C.	5 C.	6 C.
Green pepper, cut into strips	1	2	3	4	5	6
Diced tomatoes	28 oz.	56 oz.	84 oz.	112 oz.	140 oz.	168 oz.
Mustard	1 T.	2 T.	3 T.	1/4 C.	1/4 C. + 1 T.	1/4 C. + 2 T.
Worcestershire sauce	1 T.	2 T.	3 T.	1/4 C.	1/4 C. + 1 T.	1/4 C. + 2 T.
Sugar	1 T.	2 T.	3 T.	1/4 C.	1/4 C. + 1 T.	1/4 C. + 2 T.
Chili sauce	3/4 C.	1-1/2 C.	2-1/4 C.	3 C.	3-3/4 C.	4-1/2 C.
Ketchup	1 T.	2 T.	3 T.	1/4 C.	1/4 C. + 1 T.	1/4 C. + 2 T.
Fresh hot sausage	3 lb.	6 lb.	9 lb.	12 lb.	15 lb.	18 lb.
On Hand:						
Large sub buns	9	18	27	36	45	54

Assembly Directions:

Sauté the onion and green pepper in a small amount of butter or margarine or with cooking spray in a large skillet. Add the tomatoes, mustard, Worcestershire sauce, sugar, chili sauce and ketchup to the skillet. Stir to mix well and simmer until the mixture thickens. Set aside to cool. Meanwhile, cook the sausage. If it's not already cut into pieces, cut to fit the length of the buns you bought. Grill or boil the sausage. Poke holes in the sausage as you cook it to release some of the grease. Drain and cool sausage. Keep buns on-hand.

Freezing Directions:

Put cooled sausage in a 1-gallon freezer bag or rigid container. Pour cooled sauce in on top of the sausage. Seal, label and freeze.

Serving Directions:

Thaw bag overnight in the refrigerator. Spray your crock-pot with cooking spray. Dump the sausage and sauce into the crock-pot. Cook on low until heated through; 2 to 3 hours. To serve, put some of the sauce on the bun, put a sausage on the bun. Top with more sauce and some onion and pepper chunks. Enjoy!!

Comments:

This recipe is just like the Hot Sausage Sandwiches you get at the county fair!

Nutritional Info: Crock Pot Hot Sausage Sandwiches

Per Serving: 632 Calories; 38g Fat (54.5% calories from fat); 24g Protein; 47g Carbohydrate; 4g Dietary Fiber; 86mg Cholesterol; 1399mg Sodium.

Exchanges: 2 1/2 Grain (Starch); 2-1/2 Lean Meat; 1 Vegetable; 6 Fat.

Sides & Salad Recipes

- Fruit Slush
- Make Ahead Mashed Potatoes
- Creamy Italian Noodles
- White Sauces
- Crockpot Mac 'n Cheese
- Baked Corn Casserole
- Country Baked Beans
- Champagne Salad
- Seafoam Salad
- Broccoli Rice & Cheese Casserole

Sides & Salad Recipes

TIPS FOR SIDES & SALAD RECIPES

General Tips For Sides, Salads, and Misc.

- One 16 ounce can, or 10 ounces of frozen vegetables, serves three to four adults.
- 1 pound of fresh vegetables with little waste (green beans or carrots for example), or 2 pounds with shells or heavy peels (peas, beets, and winter squash for example) serves three to four adults.
- 1/2 C. is a standard serving size for mashed potatoes, baked beans and veggie casseroles.
- 1/2 cup is a standard serving size for fruit salads.
- Can and bag sizes seem to be constantly changing now. Don't fret over using a 10-3/4 oz. can of soup when the recipe calls for a 10 oz. can. Close is good enough!
- Meats may be added to many of the side dishes in this section if you want to add protein.
- The *Make-Ahead Mashed Potatoes* also serve as a good top layer to many casseroles and thick stews.
- Ham could also be added to the *Crock-Pot Mac 'n Cheese* for a great main dish.
- Many of these side dishes can be used as festive holiday dishes. Wouldn't it be great to have them ready in the freezer ahead of time?
- Do you regularly get together with friends for cook-outs or picnics through the summer? Or do you have neighbors or family who will call Sunday afternoon and say "Hey… we're gonna grill out tonite. I've got the meat, bread and some fruit… bring something else and come over!" And you say you can't, because you don't have time to make anything? If you keep a stash of stuff in the freezer for just such an occasion, you'll be so glad you did!
- Do you have church picnics, family reunions, work picnics, neighborhood block parties, etc. on your calendar already where you'll need to bring something? Take a day and make 1 or 2 things for each of the upcoming events, making the same 2

dishes for each one, if possible. That will really make it easy on you!

- If your family members can't agree on side dishes at meal time, freeze your sides in 1-2 portion containers and serve a variety.
- All fresh vegetables except chopped onion, green pepper, and celery must be blanched before being added to foods going into the freezer. See page 132 in the *Appendix* for a vegetable blanching chart.

Healthy Tips For Sides, Salads, and Misc.

- The "Lite" recipes for our nutritional information substitute skim milk for 2%, reduced fat sour cream for regular sour cream, reduced fat cheese/cottage cheese for regular cheese/cottage cheese, light cream cheese for regular cream cheese, fat free white sauce for regular white sauce, turkey bacon for bacon, light whipped topping for regular whipped topping, evaporated skim milk for half and half or regular evaporated milk and sugar-free gelatin for regular gelatin.
- Making these dishes ahead really helps to plan your "5 a day" servings of fruits and veggies!
- If you plan a potato side dish for your dinners (potatoes *are* a vegetable), a good vegetable or dark green salad, and one other raw or cooked vegetable, plus a frozen fruit salad for dessert, you will have had *four* of those servings - easy huh?

30 Day Gourmet Website Recipes & Tips

- For more great 30 Day Gourmet sides and salads recipes, check out the recipes section of our website at: www.30daygourmet.com
- For more sides and salads freezing tips and recipes from our cooks, check out the *Cooking-Sides & Salads* section of our message boards at www.30daygourmet.com

Recipe: Fruit Slush

Recipes:	1	2	3	4	5	6
Servings:	32	64	96	128	160	192
Makes:	16 C.	32 C.	48 C.	64 C.	80 C.	96 C.
Ingredients:						
Strawberries; sliced, sweetened, frozen	10 oz.	20 oz.	30 oz.	40 oz.	50 oz.	60 oz.
Fruit cocktail, in syrup	40 oz.	80 oz.	120 oz.	160 oz.	200 oz.	240 oz.
Orange juice concentrate, frozen	12 oz.	24 oz.	36 oz.	48 oz.	60 oz.	72 oz.
Pineapple; crushed, in juice	20 oz.	40 oz.	60 oz.	80 oz.	100 oz.	120 oz.
Bananas, diced	3	6	9	12	15	18

Assembly Directions:
Partially thaw strawberries so they can be separated. Mix all the ingredients together including all the juices from the canned and frozen fruits.

Freezing Directions:
Pour into suitable containers for your family such as quart-sized freezer bags, small rigid freezer containers or foil baking cups. Allow about 1/4 – 1/3 C. per child and 1/2 C. per adult. The leftovers have to be re-frozen, so make sure not to have too much leftover. Seal, label and freeze.

Serving Directions:
That 10 to 15 minutes before needed. It should be slushy.

Comments:
Fresh fruits may be added to your liking. Small Styrofoam cups with lids may be purchased at restaurant supply stores. These work well for take-out lunches. By lunchtime, they will be slushy and ready to eat.

Nutritional Info: Fruit Slush
Per Serving: 67 Calories; trace Fat (1.5% calories from fat); 1g Protein; 17g Carbohydrate; 1g Dietary Fiber; 0mg Cholesterol; 3mg Sodium.
Exchanges: 1 Fruit.

Recipe: Make Ahead Mashed Potatoes

Recipes:	1	2	3	4	5	6
Servings:	14	28	42	56	70	84
Makes:	7 C.	14 C.	21 C.	28 C.	35 C.	42 C.
Ingredients:						
Potatoes	5 lbs.	10 lbs.	15 lbs.	20 lbs.	25 lbs.	30 lbs.
Cream cheese	8 oz.	16 oz.	24 oz.	32 oz.	40 oz.	48 oz.
Eggs	1	2	3	4	5	6
Garlic powder	1/2 t.	1 t.	1-1/2 t.	2 t.	2-1/2 t.	3 t.
Salt	1 t.	2 t.	1 T.	1 T. + 1 t.	1 T. + 2 t.	2 T.
Butter or margarine, melted	3 T.	1/4 C. + 2 T.	1/2 C. + 1 T.	3/4 C.	3/4 C. + 3 T.	1 C. + 2 T.
Almonds, sliced (optional)	1/4 C.	1/2 t.	3/4 t.	1 t.	1 1/4 t.	1-1/2 t.
Paprika for color						

Assembly Directions:

Peel and quarter potatoes. Place the potatoes in a saucepan and cover completely with water. Bring to a boil, and then gently cook until tender. Drain well. In a large bowl, combine potatoes, cream cheese, egg(s), garlic powder and salt. Mash well by hand or with an electric mixer. Spoon potatoes into spray-treated or greased 3-quart casserole or 9 x 13 pan. Drizzle or brush melted butter over potatoes. Sprinkle with almonds (optional) and paprika.

Freezing Directions:

Wrap pan tightly with freezer paper, foil or place dish in a 2-gallon freezer bag. You may also put the potato mixture into a 1-gallon freezer bag adding the melted butter and almonds just before baking.

Serving Directions:

Thaw completely. Bake at 375 degrees for 30 to 40 minutes until the top is golden brown.

Comments:

You'll love having this side dish handy.

Options:

1/4 C. of crumbled, crisp bacon may be stirred in for great flavor.
Potatoes may also be topped with 1/2 C. shredded cheddar cheese.

Nutritional Info: Make Ahead Mashed Potatoes

Per Serving: 227 Calories; 10g Fat (38.4% calories from fat); 6g Protein; 30g Carbohydrate; 3g Dietary Fiber; 31mg Cholesterol; 243mg Sodium.
Exchanges: 2 Grain (Starch); 1/2 Lean Meat; 2 Fat.

Nutritional Info: Make Ahead Mashed Potatoes - Lite

Replace the cream cheese with light cream cheese. No bacon or cheese was added.
Per Serving: 207 Calories; 7g Fat (30.2% calories from fat); 6g Protein; 31g Carbohydrate; 3g Dietary Fiber; 22mg Cholesterol; 286mg Sodium.
Exchanges: 2 Grain (Starch); 1/2 Lean Meat; 1 Fat.

Nutritional information for the bacon and cheese options is available in the Members' section of our website at www.30daygourmet.com

SIDES & SALADS RECIPES

Recipe: Creamy Italian Noodles

Recipes:	1	2	3	4	5	6
Servings:	6	12	18	24	30	36
Ingredients:						
Egg noodles, wide	8 oz.	16 oz.	24 oz.	32 oz.	40 oz.	48 oz.
Butter or margarine, softened	1/4 C.	1/2 C.	3/4 C.	1 C.	1-1/4 C.	1-1/2 C.
Half and half	1/2 C.	1 C.	1-1/2 C.	2 C.	2-1/2 C.	3 C.
Parmesan cheese, grated	1/4 C.	1/2 C.	3/4 C.	1 C.	1-1/4 C.	1-1/2 C.
Italian dressing mix	1/2 envelope	1 envelope	1-1/2 envelopes	2 envelopes	2-1/2 envelopes	3 envelopes

Assembly Directions:
Cook the noodles half the time recommended on the package. Drain. Put the drained noodles in a bowl and add the butter, tossing to coat. Add the half and half, the Parmesan cheese and the dressing mix to the bowl. Stir to mix well.

Freezing Directions:
Put noodle mixture in a freezer bag or plastic container with a lid. Label, seal and freeze.

Serving Directions:
Thaw overnight in the fridge, or thaw in the microwave. Reheat in the microwave until hot, and serve. The actual reheat time will depend on your microwave.

Comments:
What a tasty quick and easy side dish!

Nutritional Info: Creamy Italian Noodles
Per Serving: 257 Calories; 12g Fat (43.8% calories from fat); 7g Protein; 29g Carbohydrate; 1g Dietary Fiber; 46mg Cholesterol; 380mg Sodium.
Exchanges: 2 Grain (Starch); 2 Fat.

Nutritional Info: Creamy Italian Noodles - Lite
Replace half and half with evaporated skim milk.
Per Serving: 247 Calories; 10g Fat (37.3% calories from fat); 8g Protein; 30g Carbohydrate; 1g Dietary Fiber; 39mg Cholesterol; 397mg Sodium.
Exchanges: 2 Grain (Starch); 1-1/2 Fat.

Recipe: White Sauce & Fat Free White Sauce

Recipes:	1	2	3	4	5	6
Servings:	**10**	**20**	**30**	**40**	**50**	**60**
Makes:	6 C.	12 C.	18 C.	24 C.	30 C.	36 C.
Ingredients:						
*Butter, margarine or cooking oil	3/4 C.	1-1/2 C.	2-1/4 C.	3 C.	3-3/4 C.	4-1/2 C.
Flour	3/4 C.	1-1/2 C.	2-1/4 C.	3 C.	3-3/4 C.	4-1/2 C.
Milk, warmed	6 C.	12 C.	18 C.	30 C.	30 C.	36 C.
Chicken or Beef Flavoring: Bouillon granules Or Bouillon cubes Or Broth powder	2 T. 6 1/4 C.	1/4 C. 12 1/2 C.	1/4 C. + 2 T. 18 3/4 C.	1/2 C. 24 1 C.	1/2 C. + 2 T. 30 1-1/4 C.	3/4 C. 36 1-1/2 C.

Assembly Directions for White Sauce:

We used to make this white sauce on the stove. All of that stirring without scorching almost drove us nuts even though the finished product was always worth it. Then we learned to do this in the microwave. Wow – easy! It's best to make it in 6-cup batches in a glass measuring cup. Just melt the butter/margarine, add flour and broth flavoring, then microwave for about 60-90 seconds until the mixture is bubbly. Add 2 C. of the milk, microwave for 2 minutes; Add 2 more C of milk, microwave for 2 minutes, etc., until there are 6 C. in the bowl. Microwave and stir in 2-minute increments until thick. A 6-cup batch will take about 15 minutes.

Assembly Directions for Fat Free White Sauce:

Since the fat free sauce has no butter, just warm up 2 cups of the milk for 60-90 seconds. Then stir the flour and broth flavoring into the warm milk. Follow the directions above.

Freezing Directions:

When combined with other foods in casseroles, etc. this sauce freezes well. We would not recommend freezing it separately.

Comments:

This is a great substitute for canned, creamed soups (1-1/2 C. of white sauce = 1 small can of soup) and saves money. If you use skim milk and canola oil, it is lower in fat and much better for your health, too. It can be seasoned with salt and pepper or other seasonings.

Optional: For more flavor and vitamins, add any of these finely minced vegetables: Sautéed or steamed onion, celery, mushrooms, or broccoli.

Optional: For a cheese sauce, just add shredded cheddar, Swiss or grated parmesan cheese in desired amounts while sauce is still hot. Stir until melted.

Nutritional Info: White Sauce

Per Serving: 232 Calories; 17g Fat (64.4% calories from fat); 6g Protein; 15g Carbohydrate; trace Dietary Fiber; 11mg Cholesterol; 456mg Sodium.
Exchanges: 1/2 Grain (Starch); 1/2 Non-Fat Milk; 3-1/2 Fat.

Nutritional Info: Fat Free White Sauce

Per Serving: 100 Calories; 1g Fat (5.0% calories from fat); 6g Protein; 17g Carbohydrate; trace Dietary Fiber; 3mg Cholesterol; 299mg Sodium.
Exchanges: 1/2 Grain (Starch); 1/2 Non-Fat Milk.

Recipe: Crock-pot Mac n' Cheese

Recipes:	1	2	3	4	5	6
Servings:	10	20	30	40	50	60
Ingredients:						
Macaroni, dry	16 oz.	32 oz.	48 oz.	64 oz.	80 oz.	96 oz.
Condensed cheddar cheese soup	10 oz.	20 oz.	30 oz.	40 oz.	50 oz.	60 oz.
Sharp cheddar cheese, grated	8 oz.	16 oz.	24 oz.	32 oz.	40 oz.	48 oz.
Extra-sharp cheddar cheese, grated	8 oz.	16 oz.	24 oz.	32 oz.	40 oz.	48 oz.
Evaporated milk	12 oz.	24 oz.	36 oz.	48 oz.	60 oz.	72 oz.
Milk	1 C.	2 C.	3 C.	4 C.	5 C.	6 C.

Assembly Directions:
Cook macaroni according to package directions. While macaroni is cooking, add soup, grated cheeses, evaporated milk, and milk to crock-pot, on low. Stir to combine. When macaroni is cooked, drain and add to crock-pot. Stir to mix. Cook on low 3 hours. Cool.

Freezing Directions:
Put into freezer bags or rigid containers, dividing it into appropriate serving sizes for your family. Seal, label and freeze.

Serving Directions:
Thaw. Spray a baking dish with cooking spray, and put thawed macaroni in it. Bake at 350 degrees for 25-30 minutes, or until heated through.

Comments:
I love all kinds of macaroni 'n cheese! This is the easiest and best I have ever made. Have it going in the crock-pot on assembly day and you can make several batches in a day.

Variations:
Mexican Mac 'n Cheese: Substitute Fiesta Nacho Cheese condensed soup for the cheddar cheese soup, and Pepper Jack cheese for the Extra-Sharp Cheddar cheese. You can also add a can of drained, chopped green chilies, if desired.

Broccoli Mac 'n Cheese: Substitute Broccoli Cheese condensed soup for the Cheddar Cheese soup.

Main Dish: I have added a cup of cooked, chopped chicken to make this a main dish for my family.

Nutritional Info: Crock-Pot Mac 'N Cheese
Per Serving: 448 Calories; 21g Fat (43.1% calories from fat); 22g Protein; 42g Carbohydrate; 1g Dietary Fiber; 67mg Cholesterol; 549mg Sodium.
Exchanges: 2-1/2 Grain (Starch); 1-1/2 Lean Meat; 1/2 Non-Fat Milk; 3 Fat.

Nutritional Info: Crock-Pot Mac 'N Cheese - Lite
Replace cheddar cheese with low fat cheddar cheese, evaporated milk with evaporated skim milk and 2% milk with skim milk.
Per Serving: 320 Calories; 6g Fat (18.1% calories from fat); 22g Protein; 43g Carbohydrate; 1g Dietary Fiber; 18mg Cholesterol; 549mg Sodium.
Exchanges: 2-1/2 Grain (Starch); 1-1/2 Lean Meat; 1/2 Non-Fat Milk; 1/2 Fat.

Nutritional information for Crock-Pot Mac 'N Cheese variations are available in the Members' section of our website at www.30daygourmet.com

Recipe: Baked Corn Casserole

Recipes:	1	2	3	4	5	6
Servings:	8	6	24	32	40	48
Makes: 8 x 8 pan	1	2	3	4	5	6
Ingredients:						
Corn Muffin mix, 8.5oz.	1	2	3	4	5	6
Sour cream	8 oz.	16 oz.	24 oz.	32 oz.	40 oz.	48 oz.
Canned corn, drained	15 oz.	30 oz.	45 oz.	60 oz.	75 oz.	90 oz.
Canned creamed corn	15 oz.	30 oz.	45 oz.	60 oz.	75 oz.	90 oz.
Egg	1	2	3	4	5	6
Margarine, melted	1/4 C.	1/2 C.	3/4 C.	1 C.	1-1/4 C.	1-1/2 C.
Shredded cheddar cheese	1 C.	2 C.	3 C.	4 C.	5 C.	6 C.

Assembly Directions:

In a large bowl, add the muffin mix, sour cream, corn, creamed corn, egg, margarine and cheddar cheese. Stir by hand until thoroughly mixed.

Freezing Directions:

Put the mixture in a gallon freezer bag. Seal, label and freeze.

Serving Directions:

Thaw bag overnight in the refrigerator. Pour into a greased 1.5 quart casserole dish, or a greased 8x8 pan. Bake at 350 degrees for 1 hour. To test for doneness, a knife inserted in the center should come out wet, but clean. Serve hot.

Comments:

What a quick and easy side dish! It's different, but everybody loves it!

Nutritional Info: Baked Corn Casserole

Per Serving: 329 Calories; 19g Fat (51.2% calories from fat); 8g Protein; 33g Carbohydrate; 2g Dietary Fiber; 51mg Cholesterol; 601mg Sodium.
Exchanges: 2 Grain (Starch); 1/2 Lean Meat; 3-1/2 Fat.

Nutritional Info: Baked Corn Casserole - Lite

Replace sour cream with reduced fat sour cream and the cheddar cheese with reduced fat cheddar cheese.
Per Serving: 246 Calories; 10g Fat (36.0% calories from fat); 8g Protein; 33g Carbohydrate; 2g Dietary Fiber; 29mg Cholesterol; 592mg Sodium.
Exchanges: 2 Grain (Starch); 1/2 Lean Meat; 1-1/2 Fat.

Recipe: Country Baked Beans

Recipes:	1	2	3	4	5	6
Servings:	8	16	24	32	40	48
Ingredients:						
Ground beef	1 lb.	2 lb.	3 lb.	4 lb.	5 lb.	6 lb.
Chopped onion	1 C.	2 C.	3 C.	4 C.	5 C.	6 C.
Pork 'n Beans	22 oz.	44 oz.	66 oz.	88 oz.	110 oz.	132 oz.
Kidney beans	15 oz.	30 oz.	45 oz.	60 oz.	75 oz.	90 oz.
Butter beans	15 oz.	30 oz.	45 oz.	60 oz.	75 oz.	90 oz.
Ketchup	1/2 C.	1 C.	1-1/2 C.	2 C.	2-1/2 C.	3 C.
Prepared mustard	1 t.	2 t.	1 T.	1 T. + 1 t.	1 T. + 2 t.	2 T.
Cider vinegar	2 t.	1 T. + 1 t.	2 T.	2 T. + 2 t.	3 T. + 1 t.	1/4 C.
Brown sugar	3/4 C.	1-1/2 C.	2-1/4 C.	3 C.	3-3/4 C.	4-1/2 C.
Bacon; cooked and crumbled	1/2 lb.	1 lb.	1-1/2 lb.	2 lb.	2-1/2 lb.	3 lb.

Assembly Directions:

Put hamburger and onion in a skillet and cook until burger starts to brown and onion is tender. Drain any grease. Set cooked burger aside. Open the cans of beans and drain the juice from each can into a large bowl. Don't add the beans yet. Add the ketchup, mustard, vinegar and brown sugar to the bowl of 'bean juice'. Stir until well mixed. (You may need to use a whisk to get the mustard mixed in.) Add the beans, the hamburger and the bacon. Stir to mix. Salt to taste, if desired.

Freezing Directions:

Put bean mixture in a one-gallon freezer bag. Seal, label and freeze.

Serving Directions:

Thaw. Put mixture into a 2-quart casserole dish. Bake at 350 degrees for 40 minutes. Serve hot.

Note: For best results, this dish really needs to bake. The flavors and textures blend during baking. If you want to serve it from the freezer with just a quick re-heat in the microwave, bake it before freezing.

Comments:

This is a wonderful dish that everyone loves! You can sprinkle a handful of grated cheddar cheese on top before serving, if desired. For a large gathering, these beans keep great in the crock-pot. Leftovers reheat great! Serve with a salad and rolls as a main dish, if desired.

Nutritional Info: Country Baked Beans

Per Serving: 423 Calories; 16g Fat (33.1% calories from fat); 26g Protein; 47g Carbohydrate; 12g Dietary Fiber; 47mg Cholesterol; 831mg Sodium.

Exchanges: 2 Grain (Starch); 2-1/2 Lean Meat; 1-1/2 Fat; 1 Other Carbohydrates.

Recipe: Champagne Salad

Recipes:	1	2	3	4	5	6
Servings:	**8**	**16**	**24**	**32**	**40**	**48**
Makes:	**8 C.**	**16 C.**	**24 C.**	**32 C.**	**40 C.**	**48 C.**
Ingredients:						
Sugar	3/4 C.	1-1/2 C.	2-1/4 C.	3 C.	3-3/4 C.	4-1/2 C.
Cream cheese	8 oz.	16 oz.	24 oz.	32 oz.	40 oz.	48 oz.
Frozen, sliced strawberries, thawed	10 oz.	20 oz.	30 oz.	40 oz.	50 oz.	60 oz.
Canned, crushed pineapple; drained	20 oz.	40 oz.	60 oz.	80 oz.	100 oz.	120 oz.
Bananas, diced	2	4	6	8	10	12
Walnuts or pecans, chopped (optional)	1 C.	2 C.	3 C.	4 C.	5 C.	6 C.
*Frozen whipped topping, thawed	10 oz.	20 oz.	30 oz.	40 oz.	50 oz.	60 oz.

Assembly Directions:

In a large mixing container, cream the sugar and cream cheese together. Add strawberries, pineapple, bananas, and nuts (optional). Mix well. Fold in the whipped topping.

Freezing Directions:

Spread in desired containers. Seal, label and freeze.

Serving Directions:

To serve, thaw small portions 10-15 minutes before cutting into squares to serve, or large portions up to 30 minutes before serving.

Comments:

*4-5 Cups of real whipped cream may be substituted for the 10 oz. container of whipped topping.
*Try your own combinations of fruit. Even drained fruit cocktail, or melon balls would be good. Raspberries and blueberries work well because of their small size.

Nutritional Info: Champagne Salad

Per Serving: 456 Calories; 28g Fat (53.2% calories from fat); 4g Protein; 51g Carbohydrate; 3g Dietary Fiber; 31mg Cholesterol; 95mg Sodium.

Exchanges: 1/2 Lean Meat; 1-1/2 Fruit; 5-1/2 Fat; 2 Other Carbohydrates.

Nutritional Info: Champagne Salad - Lite

Replaced cream cheese with light cream cheese and whipped topping with light whipped topping. Using nonfat whipped topping will reduce the calories to 369 and the fat to 14g. Most of the remaining fat in this recipe is from the pecans. Removing them will further reduce the fat content to 5g per serving.

Per Serving: 389 Calories; 18g Fat (40.2% calories from fat); 5g Protein; 56g Carbohydrate; 3g Dietary Fiber; 16mg Cholesterol; 162mg Sodium.

Exchanges: 1/2 Lean Meat; 1-1/2 Fruit; 2-1/2 Fat; 1-1/2 Other Carbohydrates.

Recipe: Seafoam Salad

Recipes:	1	2	3	4	5	6
Servings:	6	12	18	24	30	36
Makes:	6 C.	12 C.	18 C.	24 C.	30 C.	36 C.
Ingredients:						
Pear juice	1 C.	2 C.	3 C.	4 C.	5 C.	6 C.
Lime gelatin; dry	3 oz.	6 oz.	9 oz.	12 oz.	15 oz.	18 oz.
Cream cheese	8 oz.	16 oz.	24 oz.	32 oz.	40 oz.	48 oz.
Milk	2 T.	1/4 C.	1/4 C. + 2 T.	1/2 C.	1/2 C. + 2 T.	3/4 C.
Canned pears; drained and mashed (reserve juice)	29 oz. or 2-1/2 C.	58 oz. or 5 C.	87 oz. or 7-1/2 C.	116 oz. or 10 C.	145 oz. or 12-1/2 C.	174 oz. or 15 C.
Whipping cream or whipped topping	1 C.	2 C.	3 C.	4 C.	5 C.	6 C.

Assembly Directions:

Heat pear juice and mix with gelatin. Let set until slightly firm. Meanwhile, soften the cream cheese with the milk and whip the cream until stiff. Pour gelatin mixture over cream cheese. Beat with mixer until smooth. Add mashed pears. Fold in whipped cream or whipped topping.

Freezing Directions:

Pour into suitable containers. Seal, label and freeze.

Serving Directions:

Thaw completely in refrigerator. Serve cold. Refrigerate leftovers.

Comments:

You may use pears canned in juice OR syrup, sugar free OR regular gelatin, light OR regular cream cheese, and whipping cream OR whipped topping.

To mold instead of making in a container, pour into mold(s), refrigerate until firm, remove from mold and then freeze.

Nutritional Info: Seafoam Salad

Per Serving: 288 Calories; 16g Fat (49.8% calories from fat); 5g Protein; 33g Carbohydrate; 2g Dietary Fiber; 42mg Cholesterol; 160mg Sodium.

Exchanges: 1/2 Lean Meat; 1 Fruit; 3 Fat; 1 Other Carbohydrates.

Nutritional Info: Seafoam Salad - Lite

Replace regular lime gelatin with sugar-free lime gelatin, cream cheese with light cream cheese, whipped topping with light whipped topping and 2% milk with skim milk.

Per Serving: 182 Calories; 8g Fat (39.6% calories from fat); 5g Protein; 23g Carbohydrate; 2g Dietary Fiber; 21mg Cholesterol; 276mg Sodium.

Exchanges: 1/2 Lean Meat; 1 Fruit; 1 Fat.

SIDES & SALADS RECIPES

Recipe: Broccoli, Rice and Cheese Casserole

Recipes:	1	2	3	4	5	6
Servings:	12	24	36	48	60	72
Makes: 9 x 13 pan	1	2	3	4	5	6
Ingredients:						
Small onion, chopped	1	2	3	4	5	6
Butter or margarine	1/2 C.	1 C.	1-1/2 C.	2 C.	2-1/2 C.	3 C.
Canned cream of mushroom soup	10 oz.	20 oz.	30 oz.	40 oz.	50 oz.	60 oz.
Water	3/4 C.	1-1/2 C.	2-1/4 C.	3 C.	3-3/4 C.	4-1/2 C.
Cheez Whiz	8 oz.	16 oz.	24 oz.	32 oz.	40 oz.	48 oz.
On Hand:						
Minute Rice, uncooked	1-1/4 C.	2-1/2 C.	3-3/4 C.	5 C.	6-1/4 C.	7-1/2 C.
Chopped frozen broccoli, thawed	20 oz.	40 oz.	60 oz.	80 oz.	100 oz.	120 oz.

Assembly Directions:

Sauté onion in butter in a skillet or saucepan until tender. Add soup and water. Turn heat to low. Heat jar of Cheez Whiz in the microwave without the lid for 30 seconds to make it easier to get out of the jar. Add Cheez Whiz to the saucepan or skillet. Stir to mix, until cheese is melted. Set aside to cool.

Freezing Directions:

Place cheese mixture in a freezer bag. Seal, label and freeze. Keep broccoli in the freezer with the sauce mixture.

Serving Directions:

Thaw bag of cheese sauce and bag of broccoli overnight in the refrigerator. Combine sauce, broccoli and rice in a large bowl, stirring until well mixed. Dump mixture into a 9x13 pan. Bake for 20 minutes at 325 degrees. Serve hot.

Nutritional Info: Broccoli, Rice and Cheese Casserole

Per Serving: 207 Calories; 15g Fat (62.8% calories from fat); 4g Protein; 16g Carbohydrate; 2g Dietary Fiber; 10mg Cholesterol; 667mg Sodium.
Exchanges: 1/2 Grain (Starch); 1/2 Vegetable; 2 Fat.

Nutritional Info: Broccoli, Rice and Cheese Casserole - Lite

Replace cream of mushroom soup with reduced fat cream of mushroom soup and Cheez Whiz with Cheez Whiz Light.
Per Serving: 178 Calories; 10g Fat (50.5% calories from fat); 6g Protein; 17g Carbohydrate; 2g Dietary Fiber; 13mg Cholesterol; 468mg Sodium.
Exchanges: 1/2 Grain (Starch); 1/2 Vegetable; 1-1/2 Fat.

Snack & Dessert Recipes

- Granola Bars
- Freezer Pie Crust
- Freezer Pie Fillings
- Helen's Nutty Bars
- Ice Cream Shop Pie
- Pecan Pie Muffins
- Frozen Peanut Butter Bars
- Freezer Cheesecake
- Oatmeal Cookie Mix
- Teddy Bear Snack Mix

Snack & Dessert Recipes

TIPS FOR SNACK & DESSERT RECIPES

General Tips for Snacks & Desserts

- For young kids, the key to successful freezer snacks is packaging. Make it look cute and fun! Use the printed snack sized freezer bags. It's fine to use food storage bags, too, as long as all of the little bags are stored inside a freezer bag.
- Individual packaging is helpful for portion control. 2 chocolate chip cookies in a little bag, one brownie in a ziptop bag, you get the idea. We're slipping into a "super sizing" mentality here in the USA!
- It's wonderful to have a few whole cheesecakes or pies in the freezer to give to a busy friend or pull out for unexpected company. With a piece of cheesecake going for over $5 now, what a treat!
- The snacks you make at home will always be cheaper and healthier than the ones you buy pre-packaged at the store or the restaurant.
- Adults eat snacks too! Don't just plan for the kids.

Healthy Tips For Snacks and Desserts

- Nutritional information for our snacks and desserts recipes use regular cream cheese, sour cream, whipped topping, and 2% milk. "Lite" versions substitute light cream cheese for cream cheese, light sour cream for sour cream, light whipped topping for whipped topping and skim mik for 2% milk.
- Natural peanut butter is much better for us nutritionally than the regular kind. Read the labels. Most peanut butters have the peanut oil removed and hydrogenated fats pumped in.
- Honey may be used in place of corn syrup in many recipes. Honey, however, has a stronger flavor. So you might buy the lightest color or clover honey which will be the mildest.

- Unsweetened applesauce can be substituted for up to 1/2 the oil in most recipes. Just be sure the recipe is not really high in fat in the first place, or the texture of the revised recipe may be disappointing.
- Whole-wheat flour is a good substitute for white flour whenever possible. The fiber and nutrients in the whole-wheat flour are great for our bodies! In baked goods, you can use a mixture of 1/2 whole-wheat flour and 1/2 white flour. The kids rarely know the difference. If you choose to use whole-wheat flour, you need to refrigerate it if it will not be consumed within 30 days. The natural oil in the wheat germ is very perishable.
- Wheat germ is so good for all of us. It can be sprinkled into lots of recipes (cookies, breads, snack bars, etc.) without even tasting it. Try adding one tablespoon of raw or toasted wheat germ to each cup of flour or other dry ingredients.
- Try to make sure that the snacks your children eat have a redeeming nutritional value. If they are eating a snack loaded with butter or chocolate, what does it have in it that is good for the body? Oats, nuts, whole-wheat flour, raisins or other fruits can make a bad-for-you food into an acceptable food with a few added ingredients!

30 Day Gourmet Website Recipes & Tips

- For more great 30 Day Gourmet snacks and desserts recipes, check out the recipes section of our website at: www.30daygourmet.com
- For more snacks and desserts freezing tips and recipes from our cooks, check out the *Cooking-Snacks & Desserts* section of our message boards at www.30daygourmet.com
- Check out the *Freezer Desserts to Die For!* and *Freezer Cooking for Daycare Providers & Busy Parents* eBooks offered on our website for more great recipes and tips.

Recipe: Granola Bars

Recipes:	1	2	3	4	5	6
Servings:	16	32	48	64	80	96
Ingredients:						
Vegetable oil	1/3 C.	2/3 C.	1 C.	1-1/3 C.	1-2/3 C.	2 C.
Brown sugar	3/4 C.	1-1/2 C.	2-1/4 C.	3 C.	3-3/4 C.	4-1/2 C.
Honey or corn syrup	2 T.	1/4 C.	1/4 C. + 2 T.	1/2 C.	1/2 C. + 2 T.	3/4 C.
Vanilla	1 t.	2 t.	1 T.	1 T. + 1 t.	1 T. + 2 t.	2 T.
Eggs	2	4	6	8	10	12
Flour; white or whole wheat	1 C.	2 C.	3 C.	4 C.	5 C.	6 C.
Cinnamon	1 t.	2 t.	1 T.	1 T. + 1 t.	1 T. + 2 t.	2 T.
Baking powder	1/2 t.	1 t.	1-1/2 t.	2 t.	2-1/2 t.	1 T.
Salt	1/4 t.	1/2 t.	3/4 t.	1 t.	1-1/4 t.	1-1/2 t.
Oats	1-1/2 C.	3 C.	4-1/2 C.	6 C.	7-1/2 C.	9 C.
Crisp rice cereal	2 C.	4 C.	6 C.	8 C.	10 C.	12 C.
Chopped nuts or sunflower seeds	1 C.	2 C.	3 C.	4 C.	5 C.	6 C.

Assembly Directions:

In a large mixing bowl, combine the oil, brown sugar, honey or corn syrup, vanilla and eggs. Add flour, cinnamon, baking powder and salt. Mix well. With a large spoon, stir in oats, cereal, and nuts, fruits or baking chips. Spray treat a glass 9"x13" pan. Press the mixture evenly into the bottom of the pan. For chewy bars, bake at 350 degrees for 25 minutes. For crunchy bars, bake at 300 degrees until the surface is golden brown all over; about 40-50 minutes. Cool bars completely. Cut into 16 bars by slicing through the middle lengthwise, then crosswise 7 times.

Freezing Directions:

Put the bars in rigid containers or freezer bags. For quick individual servings, put each bar in a fold-top sandwich bag, and then put all the sandwich bags in a freezer bag. Seal, label and freeze.

Serving Directions:

Thaw and enjoy! Pack frozen into lunchboxes and they will be thawed "just in time". Yum!

Comments:

Up to 1 C. of baking chips or dried fruit may be added. Glass pans seemed to give the most consistent results. For chewy bars, it's important to take them out of the oven when the timer rings. If you wait until they look like they're done, you'll have crunchy bars!

Nutritional Info: Granola Bars

Per Serving: 231 Calories; 11g Fat (40.5% calories from fat); 6g Protein; 29g Carbohydrate; 4g Dietary Fiber; 23mg Cholesterol; 85mg Sodium.
Exchanges: 1-1/2 Grain (Starch); 1/2 Lean Meat; 2 Fat; 1/2 Other Carbohydrates.

Nutritional information for Granola Bar variations may be found at the Members' section of our website at www.30daygourmet.com

Recipe: Freezer Pie Crust

Recipes:	1	2	3	4	5	6
Servings:	96	192	288	384	480	576
Makes: crusts	16	32	48	64	80	96
Ingredients:						
Vegetable shortening	3 lbs.	6 lbs.	9 lbs.	12 lbs.	15 lbs.	18 lbs.
Flour	5 lbs.	10 lbs.	15 lbs.	20 lbs.	25 lbs.	30 lbs.
Ice water	3 C.	6 C.	9 C.	12 C.	15 C.	18 C.
Salt	2 T.	1/4 C.	1/4 C. + 2 T.	1/2 C.	1/2 C. + 2 T.	3/4 C.

Assembly Directions:
Mix in a very large bowl or pan. Mix flour, salt and shortening together with hands. Add ice water and mix all together until well blended. Make into 16 patties.

Freezing Directions:
Wrap individually in freezer paper and place in a large 2-gallon freezer bag. Seal, label and freeze.

Serving Directions:
Defrost desired number of crust "patties" on the counter 30 minutes or so, or in the fridge overnight. Roll between 2 sheets of waxed paper.

Comments:
These will keep for at least 1 year in the freezer. They can be used this for dessert pies as well as quiches and meat pies. It turns out perfectly every time.

Nutritional Info: Pie Crusts for the Freezer – Single Crust
Per Serving: 214 Calories; 14g Fat (61.3% calories from fat); 2g Protein; 18g Carbohydrate; 1g Dietary Fiber; 0mg Cholesterol; 134mg Sodium.
Exchanges: 1 Grain (Starch); 3 Fat.

SNACK & DESSERT RECIPES

Recipe: Apple Pie Filling

Recipes:	1	2	3	4	5	6
Servings:	6	12	18	24	30	36
Ingredients:						
Sugar	1 C.	2 C.	3 C.	4 C.	5 C.	6 C.
Salt	1 t.	2 t.	1 T.	1 T. + 1 t.	1 T. + 2 t.	2 T.
Cinnamon	1 t.	2 t.	1 T.	1 T. + 1 t.	1 T. + 2 t.	2 T.
Nutmeg	1 t.	2 t.	1 T.	1 T. + 1 t.	1 T. + 2 t.	2 T.
Flour	1-1/2 T.	3 T.	1/4 C. + 1-1/2 t.	1/4 C. + 2 T.	1/4 C. + 3-1/2 T.	1/2 C. + 1 T.
Butter or margarine	2 T.	4 T.	6 T.	8 T.	10 T.	12 T.
Cooking apples; peeled and sliced	4 C.	8 C.	12 C.	16 C.	20 C.	24 C.
Lemon juice	1/4 C.	1/2 C.	3/4 C.	1 C.	1-1/4 C.	1-1/2 C.

Assembly Directions:
Mix sugar, salt, cinnamon, nutmeg, and flour in a small bowl. With a fork, blend butter into sugar mixture until it is crumbly. Place the lemon juice in a large bowl. As you peel and slice the apples, place them in the lemon juice and toss to coat well. When all apples have been coated with the lemon juice, pour apple slices into a colander and drain well. In a large bowl, mix drained apple slices and sugar mixture.

Freezing Directions:
Put apple mixture in a labeled freezer bag or container. Remove excess air, seal and freeze.

Nutritional Info: Apple Pie Filling - 6 servings
Per Serving: 218 Calories; 4g Fat (16.4% calories from fat); trace Protein; 47g Carbohydrate; 2g Dietary Fiber; 0mg Cholesterol; 223mg Sodium. **Exchanges:** 1/2 Fruit; 1 Fat; 2 Other Carbohydrates.

Cherry Pie Filling

Recipes:	1	2	3	4	5	6
Servings:	6	12	18	24	30	36
Ingredients:						
Sugar	1 C.	2 C.	3 C.	4 C.	5 C.	6 C.
Flour	2 T.	1/4 C.	1/4 C. + 2 T.	1/2 C.	1/2 C. + 2 T.	3/4 C.
Salt	1/8 t.	1/4 t.	3/8 t.	1/2 t.	1/2 t. + 1/8 t.	3/4 t.
Butter or margarine	2 T.	1/4 C.	1/4 C. + 2 T.	1/2 C.	1/2 C. + 2 T.	3/4 C.
Sour pie cherries (Fresh or canned and drained)	4 C.	8 C.	12 C.	16 C.	20 C.	24 C.

Assembly Directions:
In a large bowl, mix sugar, flour, and salt. With a fork, mix in butter until it is crumbly. Stir in pie cherries, stirring to coat well.

Freezing Directions:
Pour cherry mixture into a labeled freezer bag or container. Remove excess air. Seal, label and freeze.

Serving Directions:
Thaw filling, pour into pie shell, and seal top crust or sprinkle with crumbs. Bake at 425 degrees for 10 minutes, and then reduce heat to 350 degrees. Bake for 30-40 minutes until browned and bubbly.

Nutritional Info: Cherry Pie Filling - 6 servings
Per Serving: 236 Calories; 4g Fat (14.6% calories from fat); 2g Protein; 51g Carbohydrate; 2g Dietary Fiber; 0mg Cholesterol; 101mg Sodium.
Exchanges: 1 Fruit; 1 Fat; 2 Other Carbohydrates.

SNACK & DESSERT RECIPES

Recipe: Helen's Nutty Bars

Recipes:	1	2	3	4	5	6
Servings:	**35**	**70**	**105**	**140**	**175**	**210**
Ingredients:						
Yellow cake mix, box	1	2	3	4	5	6
Butter or margarine	2/3 C.	1-1/3 C.	2 C.	2-2/3 C.	3-1/3 C.	4 C.
Butter or margarine	1/3 C.	2/3 C.	1 C.	1-1/3 C.	1-2/3 C.	2 C.
Eggs	1	2	3	4	5	6
Marshmallows, miniature	4 C.	8 C.	12 C.	16 C.	20 C.	24 C.
Peanut butter baking chips	10 oz.	20 oz.	30 oz.	40 oz.	50 oz.	60 oz.
Vanilla	2 t.	1 T. + 1 t.	2 T.	2 T. + 2 t.	3 T. + 1 t.	4 T.
Corn syrup	2/3 C.	1-1/3 C.	2 C.	2-2/3 C.	3-1/3 C.	4 C.
Salted peanuts, whole or chopped	12 oz.	24 oz.	36 oz.	48 oz.	60 oz.	72 oz.

Assembly Directions:

For each recipe, combine dry cake mix with 2/3 C. of the butter and an egg. Mix well and press onto a large, rimmed baking sheet, completely covering it. Bake ten minutes at 325 degrees. Sprinkle the marshmallows over the hot cake mix layer. Bake 5 minutes more at 325 degrees. Cool completely. When the baked layers are cool, melt the baking chips, vanilla, corn syrup, and remaining butter together in a microwave safe bowl on 100% power for one minute. Stir well, then heat at 100% power again for another 30 seconds. Stir well. If it is not completely melted, heat for an additional 30 seconds. Pour the melted mixture over the cooled marshmallow layer. Spread to completely cover with a rubber spatula. Sprinkle the peanuts over the surface and press them in with a spatula or the back of a spoon.

Freezing Directions:

Chill the Nutty Bars in the refrigerator until they are firm. Cut into squares. Layer the chilled bars in a rigid freezer container with double layers of waxed paper or plastic wrap in between layers of Nutty Bars. Seal, label and freeze.

Serving Directions:

Thaw to room temperature for soft bars. Serve chilled for chewy bars. Serve from the freezer for VERY chewy bars.

Comments:

My Mom made these a lot! They are a favorite of my brother and his family in Alaska and Mom wasn't beyond making up a batch and shipping them off by FedEx. Watch out! They are a bit addictive.

Nutritional Info: Helen's Nutty Bars

Per Serving: 241 Calories; 14g Fat (51.8% calories from fat); 5g Protein; 25g Carbohydrate; 1g Dietary Fiber; 6mg Cholesterol; 191mg Sodium.

Exchanges: 1/2 Lean Meat; 2-1/2 Fat; 1-1/2 Other Carbohydrates.

Recipe: Ice Cream Shop Pie

Recipes:	1	2	3	4	5	6
Servings:	6	12	18	24	30	36
Makes: pies	1	2	3	4	5	6
Ingredients:						
Cold milk	1-1/2 C.	3 C.	4-1/2 C.	6 C.	7-1/2 C.	9 C.
Instant pudding (4 serving size)	1 box	2 boxes	3 boxes	4 boxes	5 boxes	6 boxes
Whipped topping, thawed	3 C.	6 C.	9 C.	12 C.	15 C.	18 C.
Packaged chocolate or graham cracker crust	1	2	3	4	5	6

Assembly Directions:

Pour milk into a large bowl. Add pudding mix. Beat with a wire whisk until well blended. Let stand 5 minutes until slightly thickened. Fold whipped topping and Ice Cream Shop ingredients into pudding mixture. Spoon the filling into the crust.

Freezing Directions:

Cover pie and freeze until firm, about 6 hours, or overnight.

Serving Directions:

When ready to serve, remove pie from freezer. Let stand at room temperature about 10 minutes before cutting and serving. Store any leftover pie in the freezer.

Comments:

This is a very quick and easy dessert to make! You can cut it straight out of the freezer, if you don't want to wait 10 minutes for it to soften. This is a great dessert to keep in the freezer for unexpected company!

Rocky Road Pie: Use any chocolate flavored pudding mix and chocolate crumb crust. Fold in 1/2 C. each: semi-sweet chocolate chips, mini-marshmallows and chopped nuts with the whipped topping. Serve drizzled with chocolate sauce, if desired.

Toffee Bar Crunch Pie: Use French vanilla or vanilla flavored pudding mix and graham cracker crumb crust. Spread 1/3 C. butterscotch sauce in the bottom of the crust before filling. Fold in 1 C. chopped chocolate-covered English toffee bars (such as Heath) with whipped topping. Garnish with additional chopped toffee bars, if desired.

Chocolate Cookie Pie: Use French vanilla or vanilla pudding mix and graham cracker crumb crust. Fold in 1 C. chopped chocolate sandwich cookies with whipped topping.

Strawberry Banana Split Pie: Use French vanilla or vanilla pudding mix, reducing milk to 3/4 C. and adding 3/4 C. pureed sweetened strawberries. Use graham cracker crust and line the bottom with banana slices before filling with whipped topping. Garnish with whipped topping, maraschino cherries and chopped nuts.

Nutritional Info: Ice Cream Shop Pie - Plain

Calculated using vanilla pudding and graham cracker crust.

Per Serving: 366 Calories; 21g Fat (50.6% calories from fat); 5g Protein; 41g Carbohydrate; 1g Dietary Fiber; 6mg Cholesterol; 321mg Sodium.

Exchanges: 4 Fat; 2-1/2 Other Carbohydrates.

Nutrition info for the Plain Lite, Rocky Road, Toffee Crunch, Chocolate Cookie, and Strawberry Banana Split and variations can be found in the Members' section of our website at www.30daygourmet.com

SNACK & DESSERT RECIPES

Recipe: Pecan Pie Muffins

Recipes:	1	2	3	4	5	6
Servings:	10	20	30	40	50	60
Makes: muffins	10	20	30	40	50	60
Ingredients:						
Large eggs	2	4	6	8	10	12
Butter or margarine, melted	1/2 C.	1 C.	1-1/2 C.	2 C.	2-1/2 C.	3 C.
Chopped pecans	1 C.	2 C.	3 C.	4 C.	5 C.	6 C.
Brown sugar	1 C.	2 C.	3 C.	4 C.	5 C.	6 C.
Flour	1/2 C.	1 C.	1-1/2 C.	2 C.	2-1/2 C.	3 C.

Assembly Directions:
Stir together eggs and melted butter by hand. Add next 3 ingredients, stirring until well mixed. Pour batter into greased/sprayed foil baking cups. Fill 2/3 full. Bake at 350 for 25 minutes or until done. Remove from pans immediately to cool.

Freezing Directions:
Once muffins are completely cool, put in one-gallon freezer bags or a rigid freezer container. Seal, label and freeze.

Serving Directions:
When ready to eat, thaw, and warm in the microwave for about 10 or 15 seconds.

Comments:
This batter is more runny than doughy, so it just makes a mess if you bake it in paper liners rather than the foil ones. This mixes up very quick and easy!

Note: One recipe will make about 32 mini-muffins.

Nutritional Info: Pecan Pie Muffins - 10 regular
Per Serving: 244 Calories; 17g Fat (62.2% calories from fat); 3g Protein; 21g Carbohydrate; 1g Dietary Fiber; 37mg Cholesterol; 124mg Sodium.
Exchanges: 1/2 Grain (Starch); 3-1/2 Fat; 1 Other Carbohydrates.

Nutritional Info: Pecan Pie Muffins - 32 mini muffins (2 muffins per serving)
Per Serving: 152 Calories; 11g Fat (62.2% calories from fat); 2g Protein; 13g Carbohydrate; 1g Dietary Fiber; 23mg Cholesterol; 77mg Sodium.
Exchanges: 1/2 Grain (Starch); 2 Fat; 1/2 Other Carbohydrates.

Recipe: Frozen Peanut Butter Bars

Recipes:	1	2	3	4	5	6
Servings:	24	48	72	96	120	144
Ingredients:						
Butter or margarine	1 C.	2 C.	3 C.	4 C.	5 C.	6 C.
Peanut butter, creamy	2 C.	4 C.	6 C.	8 C.	10 C.	12 C.
*Graham cracker crumbs	2-1/2 C.	5 C.	7-1/2 C.	10 C.	12-1/2 C.	15 C.
Powdered sugar	1-3/4 C.	3-1/2 C.	5-1/4 C.	7 C.	8-3/4 C.	10-1/2 C.
Chocolate chips, semi-sweet or milk chocolate	2 C.	4 C.	6 C.	8 C.	10 C.	12 C.
Milk	1/3 C.	2/3 C.	1 C.	1-1/3 C.	1-2/3 C.	2 C.

Assembly Directions:

In a large saucepan, melt butter and peanut butter together. Mix well. Remove from heat. Add crumbs and powdered sugar, mixing well. Spread peanut butter mixture in a jelly roll pan (for thinner bars) or 9x13 pan (for thicker bars). Chill. When the peanut butter layer is firm, melt chocolate chips with milk over low heat. Spread over chilled peanut butter mixture. Chill again.

Freezing Directions:

Cut into serving size pieces. Wrap individually and freeze in large rigid containers or one-gallon freezer bags.

Serving Directions:

Eat straight from the freezer or thaw slightly.

Comments:

Hey, you peanut butter and chocolate lovers! It doesn't get any better than this! If you can keep from eating them, these are great to keep around for company, after school snacking and for a treat after the kids go to bed!

*We have found that we can usually buy the graham cracker crumbs for the same price as the equivalent in graham crackers. Why do the work if you don't have to?

Nutritional Info: Frozen Peanut Butter Bars

Per Serving: 323 Calories; 21g Fat (55.4% calories from fat); 7g Protein; 32g Carbohydrate; 3g Dietary Fiber; trace Cholesterol; 202mg Sodium.

Exchanges: 1/2 Grain (Starch); 1/2 Lean Meat; 4 Fat; 1-1/2 Other Carbohydrates.

Recipe: Freezer Cheesecake

Recipes:	1	2	3	4	5	6
Servings:	12	24	36	48	60	72
Crust Ingredients:						
Graham cracker crumbs	1-1/2 C.	3 C.	4-1/2 C.	6 C.	7-1/2 C.	9 C.
Sugar	2 T.	1/4 C.	1/4 C. + 2 T.	1/2 C.	1/2 C. + 2 T.	3/4 C.
Butter/margarine; melted	3 T.	6 T.	9 T.	12 T.	15 T.	18 T.
Filling Ingredients:						
Cream cheese; room temperature	24 oz.	48 oz.	72 oz.	96 oz.	120 oz.	144 oz.
Eggs	4	8	12	16	20	24
Vanilla	1 t.	2 t.	1 T.	1 T. + 1 t.	1 T. + 2 t.	2 T.
Sugar	1 C.	2 C.	3 C.	4 C.	5 C.	6 C.
Sour cream	16 oz.	32 oz.	48 oz.	64 oz.	80 oz.	96 oz.

Assembly Directions:

Preheat oven to 375 degrees. For each recipe, combine graham cracker crumbs, sugar and melted butter/margarine in a medium bowl, mixing well with a fork. Press mixture into a 9 inch spring-form pan across the bottom and just a bit up the sides. (I use my fingers!) Set the pan on a small pizza pan and refrigerate while preparing the filling. In a large bowl, beat the cream cheese until it's light and creamy. Add the eggs, vanilla and sugar. Beat until creamy. Gradually add the sour cream. Continue beating until thoroughly combined. Pour filling into crust. Bake (on pizza pan) in preheated oven 50 minutes. Tara taught me that the trick to a great cheesecake is to keep the oven door shut (no checking) and to leave the cheesecake in the oven for about 15 minutes after you have turned the oven off. This prevents the "falling and cracking" problem.

Freezing Directions:

Cool the cheesecake. Remove the metal form, wrap in plastic wrap and freeze whole in a freezer bag or flash freeze the cheesecake whole and then cut it into slices and freeze the slices individually.

Serving Directions:

Thaw, serve and enjoy!

Comments:

This truly is a "no fail" recipe. I tried lots of cheesecake recipes before I finally hit on this one several years ago. It's always great! Top with fruit or chocolate syrup.

Nutritional Info: Freezer Cheesecake

Per Serving: 444 Calories; 33g Fat (66.0% calories from fat); 8g Protein; 30g Carbohydrate; trace Dietary Fiber; 141mg Cholesterol; 303mg Sodium.

Exchanges: 1/2 Grain (Starch); 1 Lean Meat; 6 Fat; 1-1/2 Other Carbohydrates.

Nutritional Info: Freezer Cheesecake - Lite

Replace cream cheese with light cream cheese and sour cream with light sour cream.

Per Serving: 309 Calories; 16g Fat (46.3% calories from fat); 9g Protein; 33g Carbohydrate; trace Dietary Fiber; 97mg Cholesterol; 444mg Sodium.

Exchanges: 1/2 Grain (Starch); 1 Lean Meat; 2-1/2 Fat; 1-1/2 Other Carbohydrates.

SNACK & DESSERT RECIPES

Recipe: Oatmeal Cookie Mix

Recipes:	1	2	3	4	5	6
Servings:	144 cookies	288 cookies	432 cookies	576 cookies	720 cookies	864 cookies
Makes:	**16 C.**	**32 C.**	**48 C.**	**64 C.**	**80 C.**	**96 C.**
Ingredients:						
Flour	3 C.	6 C.	9 C.	12 C.	15 C.	18 C.
Brown sugar	1-1/2 C.	3 C.	4-1/2 C.	6 C.	7-1/2 C.	9 C.
Granulated sugar	1-1/2 C.	3 C.	4-1/2 C.	6 C.	7-1/2 C.	9 C.
Salt	2 t.	1 T. + 1 t.	2 T.	2 T. + 2 t.	3 T. + 1 t.	1/4 C.
Baking soda	2 t.	1 T. + 1 t.	2 T.	2 T. + 2 t.	3 T. + 1 t.	1/4 C.
Baking powder	1 t.	2 t.	1 T.	1 T. + 1 t.	1 T. + 2 t.	2 T.
Shortening	2 C.	4 C.	6 C.	8 C.	10 C.	12 C.
Oats (any kind)	6 C.	12 C.	18 C.	24 C.	30 C.	36 C.
On Hand for Cookies: eggs & vanilla						

Assembly Directions:

In large bowl, mix flour, brown sugar, sugar, salt, baking soda and baking powder by hand. Cut in shortening with a pastry blender. Stir in rolled oats until mixture is evenly combined.

Freezing Directions:

Get out four 1-quart freezer bags and measure 4 C. of the cookie mix into each bag. To measure it, lightly spoon the mixture into the measuring cup… do not pack it in the cup. Each bag of cookie mix will make 3 dozen cookies. Seal, label and freeze.

Cooking Directions:

Remove a bag of cookie mix from the freezer. Allow it to come to room temperature. Dump the mix into a large bowl and add 2 eggs and 2 t. vanilla. If you are going to mix up more than 1 bag at a time, add 2 eggs and 2 t. vanilla for each bag of mix used. Stir until well mixed. The cookie dough will be very thick. You can add 1 C. total of chopped nuts, raisins, sunflower seeds, chocolate chips, etc. to the dough. You can also add 1 t. cinnamon if desired. Drop by teaspoonfuls onto baking sheets. Bake at 350 degrees for 10 to 12 minutes.

Comments:

The important thing to remember with this recipe is that **4 C. mix + 2 eggs + 2 t. vanilla = cookie dough to make 3 dozen cookies.** You can freeze the mix as directed above, or you can bake the cookies and freeze them, or you can mix up the cookie dough (with the eggs and vanilla) and freeze it in a lump or flash freeze it in balls for individual cookies. Having this mix made up puts fresh-baked cookies in your families' hands in just a few minutes. It's SO easy!!

Nutritional Info: Oatmeal Cookie Mix
Per Serving: 62 Calories; 3g Fat (44.6% calories from fat); 1g Protein; 8g Carbohydrate; trace Dietary Fiber; 0mg Cholesterol; 51mg Sodium.
Exchanges: 1/2 Grain (Starch); 1/2 Fat.

Nutritional Info: Oatmeal Cookies - 1 cookie per serving
Per Serving: 66 Calories; 3g Fat (45.4% calories from fat); 1g Protein; 8g Carbohydrate; trace Dietary Fiber; 10mg Cholesterol; 54mg Sodium.
Exchanges: 1/2 Grain (Starch); 1/2 Fat.

Recipe: Teddy Bear Snack Mix

Recipes:	1	2	3	4	5	6
Servings:	**24**	**48**	**72**	**96**	**120**	**144**
Makes:	**12 C.**	**24 C.**	**36 C.**	**48 C.**	**60 C.**	**72 C.**
Ingredients:						
Instant ramen noodles, coarsely crushed	2 C.	4 C.	6 C.	8 C.	10 C.	12 C
Golden Graham's cereal	5 C.	10 C.	15 C.	20 C.	25 C.	30 C.
Teddy Graham cookies	3 C.	6 C.	9 C.	12 C.	15 C.	18 C.
Sliced almonds or unsalted peanuts	1 C.	2 C.	3 C.	4 C.	5 C.	6 C.
Raisins	1 C.	2 C.	3 C.	4 C.	5 C.	6 C.
Ground cinnamon	1/2 t.	1 t.	1-1/2 t.	2 t.	2-1/2 t.	1 T.
Butter or margarine, softened	1/3 C.	2/3 C.	1 C.	1-1/3 C.	1-2/3 C.	2 C.
Honey	1/3 C	2/3 C.	1 C.	1-1/3 C.	1-2/3 C.	2 C.
Orange juice or water	1 t.	2 t.	1 T.	1 T. + 1 t.	1 T. + 2 t.	2 T.

Assembly Directions:

Preheat oven to 375 degrees. Remove seasoning packet from package of ramen noodles and either discard or save for another use. In a large bowl, combine the cereal, cookies, noodles, nuts, and raisins. In a small pan, combine the cinnamon, butter, honey, and juice or water. Stir over low heat until melted and well mixed. Pour the butter mixture over the snack mixture and toss gently until evenly coated. Spread each single recipe on a large rimmed baking sheet and heat in the oven for 10 minutes. Remove from the oven and cool to room temperature.

Freezing Directions:

Place the cooled snack mix in a large freezer bag or containers, or package into individual serving size portions. Remove excess air. Seal, label and freeze.

Serving Directions:

Thaw and enjoy!

Nutritional Info: Teddy Bear Snack Mix

Calculated using almonds and orange juice.
Per Serving: 319 Calories; 10g Fat (28.3% calories from fat); 4g Protein; 54g Carbohydrate; 2g Dietary Fiber; 0mg Cholesterol; 605mg Sodium.
Exchanges: 1/2 Grain (Starch); 1/2 Fruit; 1 Fat; 1/2 Other Carbohydrates.

Appendix

- **Multiplication Chart for Recipes**

- **Equivalency Charts**

- **Freezing Time Chart**

- **Blanching Chart for Vegetables**

- **Cooking Terms & Definitions**

- **Freezer Selection & Maintenance**

- **Freezer Installment & Cleaning**

- **Power Failure!**

- **Nutritional Information for Lite Recipes**

- **Index**

- **Customer Order Form**

Multiplication Chart For Recipes

1	2	3	4	5	6
1/8 tsp	1/4 tsp	1/4 + 1/8 tsp	1/2 tsp	1/2 + 1/8 tsp	3/4 tsp
1/4 tsp	1/2 tsp	3/4 tsp	1 tsp	1 1/4 tsp	1 1/2 tsp
1/2 tsp	1 tsp	1 1/2 tsp	2 tsp	2 1/2 tsp	1 T.
1 tsp	2 tsp	1 T	1 T + 1 tsp	1 T + 2 tsp	2 T
1 1/8 tsp	2 1/4 tsp	1 T + 3/8 tsp	1 T + 1 1/2 tsp	1 T+2 1/2tsp+1/8tsp	2 T + 3/4 tsp
1 1/4 tsp	2 1/2 tsp	1 T + 3/4 tsp	1 T + 2 tsp	2 T + 1/4 tsp	2 T + 1 1/2 tsp
1 1/2 tsp	1 T	1 T + 1 1/2 tsp	2 T	2 T + 1 1/2 tsp	3 T
2 tsp	1 T + 1 tsp	2 T	2 T + 2 tsp	3 T + 1 tsp	1/4 C.

1	2	3	4	5	6
1 T	2 T	3 T	1/4 c	1/4 c + 1 T	1/4 c + 2 T
1 1/2 T	3 T	1/4 c + 1 1/2 tsp	1/4 c + 2 T	1/4 C + 3 1/2 T	1/2 c + 1 T
2 T	1/4 c	1/4 c + 2 T	1/2 c	1/2 c + 2 T	3/4 c
2 1/2 T	1/3 c	1/4 c + 3 1/2 T	1/2 c + 2 T	3/4 c + 1 1/2 tsp	3/4 c + 3 T
3 T	1/4 c + 2 T	1/2 c + 1 T	3/4 c	3/4 c + 3 T	1 c + 2 T
3 1/2 T	1/4 c + 3 T	2/3 c	3/4 c + 2 T	1 c + 1 1/2 T	1 1/3 c

1	2	3	4	5	6
1/4 c	1/2 c	3/4 c	1 c	1 1/4 c	1 1/2 c
1/3 c	2/3 c	1 c	1 1/3 c	1 2/3 c	2 c
1/2 c	1 c	1 1/2 c	2 c	2 1/2 c	3 c
2/3 c	1 1/3 c	2 c	2 2/3 c	3 1/3 c	4 c
3/4 c	1 1/2 c	2 1/4 c	3 c	3 3/4 c	4 1/2 c
1 c	2 c	3 c	4 c	5 c	6 c
1 1/4 c	2 1/2 c	3 3/4 c	5 c	6 1/4 c	7 1/2 c
1 1/3 c	2 2/3 c	4 c	5 1/3 c	6 2/3 c	8 c
1 1/2 c	3 c	4 1/2 c	6 c	7 1/2 c	9 c
1 2/3 c	3 1/3 c	5 c	6 2/3 c	8 c	9 2/3 c
1 3/4 c	3 1/2 c	5 1/4 c	7 c	8 3/4 c	10 1/2 c
2 c	4 c	6 c	8 c	10 c	12 c
2 1/4 c	4 1/2 c	6 3/4 c	9 c	11 1/4 c	13 1/2 c
2 1/2 c	5 c	7 1/2 c	10 c	12 1/2 c	15 c
2 2/3 c	5 1/3 c	8 c	10 2/3 c	13 1/3 c	16 c
2 3/4 c	5 1/2 c	8 1/4 c	11 c	13 3/4 c	16 1/2 c
3 c	6 c	9 c	12 c	15 c	18 c
3 1/4 c	6 1/2 c	9 3/4 c	13 c	16 1/4 c	19 1/2 c
3 1/3 c	6 2/3 c	10 c	13 1/3 c	16 2/3 c	20 c
3 1/2 c	7 c	10 1/2 c	14 c	17 1/2 c	21 c
3 2/3 c	7 1/3 c	11 c	14 2/3 c	18 1/3 c	22 c
3 3/4 c	7 1/2 c	11 1/4 c	15 c	18 3/4 c	22 1/2 c
4 c	8 c	12 c	16 c	20 c	24 c

1	2	3	4	5	6
4 1/4 c	8 1/2 c	12 3/4 c	17 c	21 1/4 c	25 1/2 c
4 1/3 c	8 2/3 c	13 c	17 1/3 c	21 2/3 c	26 c
4 1/2 c	9 c	13 1/2 c	18 c	22 1/2 c	27 c
4 2/3 c	9 1/3 c	14 c	18 2/3 c	23 1/3 c	28 c
4 3/4 c	9 1/2 c	14 1/4 c	19 c	23 3/4 c	28 1/2 c
5 c	10 c	15 c	20 c	25 c	30 c

Equivalency Chart

DRY MEASURE

Pinch = a little less than 1/4 teaspoon
3 teaspoons = 1 Tablespoon
2 T. = 1 oz. = 1/8 C.
4 T. = 2 oz. = 1/4 C.
5-1/3 T. = 2.7 oz. = 1/3 C.
8 T. = 4 oz. = 1/2 C.
10-2/3 T. = 5.4 oz. = 2/3 C.
12 T. = 6 oz. = 3/4 C.
16 T. = 8 oz. = 1 C.
4 C. = 1 quart
4 quarts = 1 gallon
16 oz. = 1 lb.

LIQUID MEASURE

a dash = a few drops
3 teaspoons = 1 Tablespoon
2 T. = 1 oz.
4 T. = 2 oz. = 1/4 C.
5-1/3 T. = 2.7 oz. = 1/3 C.
8 T. = 4 oz. = 1/2 C.
10-2/3 T. = 6 oz. = 3/4 C.
16 T. = 8 oz. = 1 C.
2 C. = 1 pint = 1/2 quart
4 C. = 2 pints = 1 quart
4 quarts = 16 C. = 1 gallon = 128 oz.

Bread Cubes and Crumbs

4 slices of bread = 2 C. fresh soft crumbs
4 slices of bread = 3/4 C. dry crumbs
6 oz. dried bread crumbs = 1 scant cup
16 oz. loaf = 14 C. one inch cubes

Cereal

21 oz. box corn flake cereal = 7 cups
2 C. flakes = 3/4 C. crumbs
15 oz. box crisp rice = 11 cups of cereal
13 oz. box of crisp rice = 6 C. crumbs
42 oz. box rolled oats = 10 C.

Flours/Meal

1 lb. white flour = 3-1/2 C. or 4 C. sifted
1 lb. whole wheat flour = 3-1/4 C. or 3-1/2 sifted
1 C. flour = 4 oz.
14 oz. cracker meal = 3-3/4 C.

Leavening Agents

16 oz. baking soda = 2-1/3 C. = 37 T.
16 oz. baking powder = 2-1/3 C. = 37 T.
14 oz. can baking powder = 1-3/4 C. = 28 T.
5-1/2 oz. baking powder = 1 C.
.25 oz. active dry yeast = 1 T.
1 oz. of active dry yeast = 3-1/3 T.
16 oz. of active dry yeast = 3-1/3 C.
.60 oz. compressed yeast = 4 t.

Cracker & Cookie Crumbs

28 soda or saltine crackers = 1 C. fine crumbs
16 oz. crackers = 6 C. fine crumbs
15 square graham crackers = 1 C. crumbs
16 oz. graham crackers = 70 crackers
1 roll of snack crackers = about 1-1/3 C. crumbs
16 oz. of snack crackers = about 5-1/3 C. crumbs
24 round butter crackers = 1 C. fine crumbs
14 oz. box of cracker meal = 3-3/4 C. crumbs
22 vanilla wafers = 1 C. crumbs
14 Oreos (with middle) = 1 C. crumbs

Butter/Margarine/Shortening

1 T. = 1/2 oz. = 1/8 stick
4 T. = 2 oz. = 1/4 C. = 1/2 stick
8 T. = 4 oz. = 1/2 C. = 1 stick
16 T. = 8 oz. = 1 C. = 2 sticks
32 T. = 16 oz. = 2 C. = 4 sticks = 1 lb.
3 lb. can of shortening = 6 C.

Sweeteners

12 oz. honey = 1 C.
16 oz. honey = 1-1/2 C.
16 oz. corn syrup = 1-1/2 C.
11 oz. molasses = 1 C.
11 oz. maple syrup = 1 C.
16 oz. white sugar = 2-1/3 C.
4 lbs. white sugar = 10 C.
16 oz. brown sugar = 2-1/4 C. packed
16 oz. powdered sugar = 3-1/2 C.

Equivalency Chart

DAIRY PRODUCTS

Shredded and Cubed Cheese
16 oz. = 4 C. cubed or shredded
4 oz. = 1 C. cubed or shredded
Heavy Whipping Cream
1 C. or 8 oz. carton = 2 C. whipped
Parmesan or Romano Cheese, grated
6 oz. = 1 C.
16 oz. = 2-2/3 C.
24 oz. = 3 C.
Cottage Cheese
6 oz. = 1 C.
16 oz. = 2-2/3 C.
Sour Cream
16 oz. = 1-3/4 C.
9 oz. = 1 C.
Cream Cheese
3 oz. = 6 T. or about 1/3 C.
8 oz. = 1 C.
1 lb. or 16 oz. = 2 C.
Sweetened condensed milk
14 oz. can = 1-1/4 C.
Evaporated Milk
14-1/2 oz. can = 1-2/3 C.
6 oz. = 2/3 C.
Dry milk powder
16 oz. = 4 cups dry or 4-5 quarts of liquid
Buttermilk Powder
12 oz. = 3-3/4 qts. of liquid buttermilk
1/4 C. buttermilk powder = 1 C. buttermilk

FRUITS

Apples
1 lb. = 3 medium
1 medium = 1 C. chopped
Applesauce
16 oz. = 2 C.
Bananas
1 lb. = 3 med. = 2-1/2 C. diced or 3 C. sliced
1 medium = 1/3 C. mashed
Strawberries/Raspberries
1 lb. = 2 C. sliced
Blueberries
1 lb. = 3 C.
Cranberries
1 lb. = 4 C.
Limes
1 medium = 1-1/2 to 2 T. fresh juice
Raisins
1 lb. = 3-1/2 C.
6 oz. = about 1 C.
Pineapple
1 lb. = 2-1/2 C. diced
Lemons
1 medium = 3 T. juice or 1 T. grated rind
5-8 lemons = 1 C. fresh juice
Oranges
1 = 1/3 C. fresh juice

MEATS

Bacon
8 slices = 1/2 C. cooked and crumbled
16 oz. = about 18 slices
Beef
1 lb. ground = 2-1/2 C. browned
10 lbs. ground = 25 C. browned
1 lb. beef cuts = 3-1/2 C. sliced
Bulk Sausage
1 lb. raw = 2-1/2 C. cooked and crumbled
Chicken, boneless, skinless
7-1/2 lbs. raw = about 25 pieces
1 lb. raw = 2 C. raw ground = 2-2/3 C. raw diced
5 lbs. raw = 12 C. cooked, diced
1 large breast = 3/4 C. cooked, diced
2-1/2 lbs. = 7-8 large pieces
Chicken Thighs
5 lbs. = about 25 pieces
Whole Chicken
2-1/2 lb. chicken = 2-1/2 C. cooked, diced meat
3-1/2 to 4 lb. chicken = 4 C. cooked, diced meat
4-1/2 to 5 lb. chicken = 6 C. cooked, diced meat
Crab meat (real or imitation)
1 lb. cooked and boned meat = 2 cups
Ham
1 lb. whole ham = 2-1/2 C. ground ham
1 lb. whole ham = 3 C. cubed
Turkey Breast
5 lb. raw breast = 10 C. cooked, diced meat
1 lb. drumstick or thigh = 1-1/8 C. diced
Whole Turkey
Each pound of turkey = approx. 1 C. cooked meat
Tuna Fish
6 oz. = 3/4 C. lightly packed

MISCELLANEOUS

Jams/Jellies/Preserves
6 oz. = 2/3 C.
10 oz. = about 1 C.
16 oz. = 94 t. = 32 T. = 2 C.
Nuts
16 oz. = 4 C.
oz. =   C. chopped fine
2 oz. = 1/2 C.
Cocoa Powder
8 oz. = 2 C.
16 oz. = 4 C.
Chocolate Chips
6 oz. = 1 C.
Shredded Coconut
16 oz. = 5 C.
Peanut Butter
16 oz. = 1-3/4 C.
Ice Cubes
11 cubes = 1 C. liquid
Mayonnaise
1 quart = 32 oz. = 4 C.
Marshmallows
16 oz. = 9 C.

Equivalency Chart

ONE OUNCE OF WEIGHT TO MEASUREMENT OF HERBS AND SPICES

Allspice, ground	5-1/2 T.	Mustard; dry, ground	6 T. + 1 t.
Basil	1/2 C.	Nutmeg; ground	5 T.
Bay leaf, whole	7 T.	Onion powder	4-1/2 T.
Black pepper; ground	1/2 C.	Oregano 6 T.	
Celery Seed	1/4 C.	Paprika	5 T.
Chili Pepper	1/2 C. + 1-1/2 t.	Parsley flakes	1/2 C. + 1-1/2 t.
Cinnamon	5-1/2 T.	Poppy Seeds	3-3/4 T.
Cloves, ground	5-1/2 T.	Red pepper flakes	1/2 C. = 1-1/2 t.
Cumin seed	6 T.	Rosemary	1/2 C.
Curry powder	5-1/2 T.	Sage	1/2 C. + 1-1/2 T.
Dill Weed	6 T.	Savory	6-3/4 T.
Dill Seed	4-1/2 T.	Sesame Seed	5 T.
Garlic powder	6-1/3 T.	Tarragon 6-3/4 T.	
Ginger	6 T.	Thyme	6-1/3 T.
Marjoram	1/2 C.	Turmeric	5 T.

VEGETABLES

Carrots
1 lb. = 3 C. sliced = 2 C. diced = 6-8 medium
1 medium carrot = 1/2 C. grated
Cooking Onions
1 lb. = 3 medium = 3 C. sliced or chopped
1 medium onion = 1 C. chopped = 2/3 C. sauteed
Green Onion 7 medium green onions = 1/2 C. sliced
Green Beans
1 lb. fresh = 3 C. = 2-1/2 C. cooked
Green Pepper 1 large = 1 C. diced
Broccoli 1 lb. fresh or frozen = 2 C. flowerets
Cabbage 1 lb. = 4 C. shredded
Cauliflower 1 lb. = 1-1/2 C. cooked = 3 C. florets
Celery
1 medium bunch = 2-1/2 to 3 C. sautéed
1 medium bunch = 3 C. diced = 3-1/2 C. sliced
3 large ribs = about 1-1/2 C. diced
1 Cup diced = 2/3 C. sautéed
1 rib = 1/2 C. sliced or diced
Corn
2-3 fresh ears = 1 C. kernels
1 lb. frozen = 3 C. kernels
Peas 4 oz. = 1 C.
Potatoes
1 lb. = 3 medium = 2-3/4 C. diced = 3 C. sliced
1 lb. = 2 C. mashed
5 lbs. = 10 C. diced or mashed
Sweet Potatoes
1 lb. = 3 medium = 2 1/2 - 3 diced
Spinach and other greens
1 lb. raw = 10-12 C. torn = 1 C. cooked
10 oz. frozen = 1-1/2 lb. fresh = 1-1/2 C. cooked
Sweet Bell Peppers
1 medium = 1/2 C. finely chopped
1 lb. = 5 medium or 3-1/2 C. diced
Mushrooms
4 oz. fresh = 1 C. whole = 1/2 C. cooked
1 lb. = about 20 large or 40 medium whole
Tomatoes 1 lb. = 4 small = 1-1/2 C. cooked
Garlic 1 medium clove = 1/2 t. minced
Water Chestnuts 8 oz. sliced or whole = 1 C. drained

DRY BEANS/GRAINS/PASTA/NUTS

Lentils
6 oz. dry = 1 C.
Kidney Beans
11 oz. dry = 1 C. dry = 3 C. cooked
15 oz. can = 1-3/4 C.
16 oz. dry = 5 C. cooked
Barley
3/4 C. pearl barley = 3 C. cooked
1 C. quick cooking barley = 2-1/2 C. cooked
Long Grain White Rice
16 oz. dry = 2-1/2 C. dry = 10 C. cooked
1 C. dry = 7 oz. dry = 3 C. cooked
Quick Cooking Brown Rice
1 C. dry = 2 C. cooked
12 oz. box = 5-1/3 C. fully cooked
       = 4-1/2 C. half cooked
White Converted Rice
1 C. dry = 4 C. cooked
Oatmeal
42 oz. dry = 10 C. dry
Spaghetti
2 oz. = 1 serving = 1/2" diameter dry portion
16 oz. = 4-5 C. dry = 10 C. cooked
Elbow Macaroni
4 oz. dry = 1 C. dry = 2-1/2 C. cooked
16 oz. dry = 4 C. dry = 9 C. cooked
Egg Noodles
4 oz. dry = 1 C. dry = 3 C. cooked
16 oz. dry = 4 C. dry = 12 C. cooked
Tiny Pasta (acini pepe, orzo, ditalini, alphabets)
8 oz. dry = 1-1/3 C. dry

Freezing Time Chart

The following list should give you a good idea of the basics when freezing most ingredients used in **30 DAY GOURMET** cooking. Remember, nothing goes "bad" in the freezer. It may just lose quality over time. Packaging makes all the difference. To determine how long to freeze a recipe that has a combination of different ingredients, the item that freezes well the least amount of time is how long to freeze the entire recipe.

FOOD	FREEZER LIFE
Baked Goods:	
Bread dough; yeast, unbaked	2 weeks
Baked bread	12 months
Rolls:	
unbaked	2 weeks
1/2 baked	12 months
fully baked	12-15 months
Muffins:	
unbaked	2 weeks
baked	3 months
Waffle/pancake batter	2-4 weeks
Waffles/pancakes, cooked	6 months
Dairy Products:	
Butter:	
salted	3 months
unsalted	6 months
Margarine	5 months
Hard cheese	3 months
Cream cheese	3 months
Milk	1 month
Eggs, raw and out of shell	6 month
Produce:	
All Vegetables	12 months
Exceptions:	
Asparagus	8-12 months
Onions	6 months
Jerusalem artichokes	3 months
Potatoes	3-6 months
Beets	6 months
Green beans	8-12 months
Leeks	6 months
Winter squash	10 months
Mushrooms	8 months
Corn on the Cob	8-10 months
Herbs	6 months
Vegetable Purees	6-12 months
Prepared Vegetable Dishes	3 months
Miscellaneous:	
Pasta, cooked	3-4 months
Pasta, mixed into dishes	3-4 months
Rice, cooked	3-4 months
Rice, mixed into dishes	3-4 months

FOOD	FREEZER LIFE
Beef:	
raw ground beef/stew beef	3-4 months
fresh beef steak	6-12 months
fresh beef roast	6-12 months
fresh beef sausage	3-4 months
smoked beef links or patties	1-2 months
cooked beef dishes	2-3 months
fresh beef in marinade	2-3 months
Pork:	
ground pork	3-4 months
fresh pork sausage	1-2 months
fresh pork chops	4-6 months
fresh pork roast	4-6 months
bacon	1 month
pepperoni	1-2 months
smoked pork links or patties	1-2 months
canned ham	don't freeze
ham, fully cooked	
whole:	1-2 months
half or slices:	1-2 months
pre-stuffed pork chops	don't freeze
cooked pork chops	2-4 months
uncooked casseroles w/ham	1 month
cooked casseroles w/ham	1 month
fresh pork in marinade	2-3 months
Poultry:	
fresh ground turkey	2-3 months
fresh turkey sausage	1-2 months
fresh whole turkey	12 months
chicken or turkey:	
fresh pieces	9 months
cooked pieces	4 months
cooked nuggets	3-4 months
pre-stuffed chicken breasts	don't freeze
cooked poultry dishes	4-6 months
fresh chicken in marinade	2-3 months
Fish:	
fresh pieces	6-12 months
cooked pieces	2-3 months
cooked fish dishes	2-3 months
fish in marinade	2-3 months
Miscellaneous:	
vegetable or meat soups/stews	2-3 months
ground veal and lamb	3-4 months
gravy and meat broths	2-3 months
cooked meat pies	3-4 months
cooked meatloaf	1-3 months

Blanching Chart For Vegetables

Always choose good, quality, fresh vegetables. Clean and trim off inedible parts. Cut to desired uniformly sized pieces.

MICROWAVE BLANCHING

- Choose a round microwaveable bowl or container.
- Place 1/4 C. of water in the container.
- Into the container, place no more than 4 C. of leafy vegetables (like spinach) or 2 C. of other vegetables.
- Cover the container with microwaveable plastic wrap.
- Make sure that if you have a turntable, it can move freely.
- Microwave according to the chart below on highest power setting.
- After blanching, spread vegetables out in a single layer on a tray or baking sheet and cool 5 minutes. They are now suitable for freezing by themselves, or in a freezer recipe.

STOVE TOP STEAMING

- Prepare vegetable as above.
- Use a pan that a wire mesh basket or steamer basket will fit into (at least 8 qt. size).
- Bring 1 inch of water to a rolling boil in the pan.
- Place no more than 1 pound of vegetables in the basket and place over the steaming water.
- Time according to the chart below.
- Remove the basket of vegetables from the pot and plunge into cold or ice water, or run cold water over them. This stops the cooking action.
- Drain well. The vegetables are now ready for freezing or using in a freezer recipe.

BOILING WATER BLANCHING

- Clean and prepare vegetables as above.
- In a large pot, bring at least 1 gallon of water for every pound of vegetables to a rolling boil.
- Plunge the vegetables in the water 1 pound at a time.
- When the water begins to boil again, start timing according to the chart below.
- At the end of the blanching time, remove vegetables from the water with a slotted spoon, steamer basket, or strainer with a handle.
- Cool hot vegetables as for range top steaming. The vegetables are now ready for use in the freezer.

BLANCHING CHART			
VEGETABLE	MICRO-STEAM	RANGE TOP STEAM	BOILING WATER
beets	n/a	n/a	30-45 min.
broccoli	5 min.	3-5 min.	2-4 min.
brussels sprouts	4 min.	6 min.	4 min.
cabbage wedges	3 min.	4 min.	3 min.
carrots	2-5 min.	4-5 min.	2-5 min.
cauliflower	5 min.	5 min.	3 min.
celery	3 min.	4 min.	3 min.
corn on the cob	n/a	n/a	6-8 min.
corn cut from cob	4 min.	6 min.	4 min.
green beans	3 min.	4 min.	3 min.
peas, all types	4 min.	6 min.	4 min.
potatoes, cut	10 min.	12 min.	10 min.
spinach/other greens	n/a	3 min.	2 min.
sweet potatoes	Any method will work. Cook until soft.		
zucchini, cubed	2-3 min	2-3 min	2-3 min
NO BLANCHING NEEDED FOR: mushrooms, onions, peppers, tomatoes, shredded zucchini			

Cooking Terms & Definitions

One of the goals of this manual is for it to be so simple that only the most basic cooking skills are needed. If you are unfamiliar with any of the cooking terms used in this manual, you should be able to find their meanings written below:

Baste: Refers to spooning or brushing juices, pan drippings, stock, broth, butter, oil or marinade over meats, poultry or fish. You can use a brush, bulb syringe, bulb baster, or spoon for this job.

Beat: This means to mix rapidly to make a mixture smooth and light. In beating, air is incorporated into the mixture. Beating by hand should be done with a whisk, a fork, or a wooden spoon. Use your wrist in a quick up and down circular motion. An electric mixer is one of the greatest cooking tools! Use a round bowl for beating, not a square or rectangular container. You will not get the corners mixed adequately.

Blanch: This means to boil rapidly in a good quantity of water. It destroys harmful enzymes in vegetables, helps to make peeling tomatoes or fruits easier, sets the color, and seals in juices and vitamins. See the blanching chart on page 133 for more complete instructions.

Blend: This means to mix two or more ingredients together so thoroughly that they become one product. This is most completely done with an electric blender or mixer.

Boil: This means to heat a liquid until bubbles constantly come to the surface. A slow boil means the bubbles lazily come to the surface. In a hard boil, the bubbles are large and rapidly break the surface.

Broil: Broiling is a cooking method using intense heat on one side. Broiling can be done in the stove, or on a grill. It is usually a quick cooking method that needs to be watched carefully to prevent burning.

Brown: The purpose of browning is to quickly sear the meat, sealing in juices and giving color to the food. Medium to high heat is usually used. Sometimes the heat is lowered to complete the cooking!

Broth: This is a liquid containing the flavors and aroma of chicken, beef, fish, or vegetables. The meat or vegetables are simmered in water, then the solids are strained out, leaving broth. Broth may be made from purchased granules or cubes that have been dissolved in water. Condensed broth is also available.

Chop: Chopping is cutting a solid object into pieces with a sharp knife. To chop efficiently, hold the blade of a large knife at both ends, bringing it up and down firmly over the food to be chopped.

Cream: This means to beat two or more ingredients together until smooth and creamy.

Cut in: Work butter, shortening, margarine, or lard into a flour mixture until it looks like coarse crumbs.

De-grease: Removing grease or fat from a broth, soup, or sauce is called de-greasing. You can skim the fat off the top with a spoon or skimmer, or chill the liquid until the fat rises to the surface and hardens. The hard fat can be removed with a slotted spatula and discarded.

Dice: This is similar to chopping, but it usually results in fairly small pieces.

Dredge: This usually means to drag a solid food like meat, fruit, or vegetables through other dry ingredients like sugar or flour. This presses the dry ingredients into the food.

Drippings: These are the juices, fats, and browned bits of food left in a pan after cooking. The drippings are good for making sauces and gravies.

Flash Freeze: or Open Freeze. To firm up foods before fully freezing by putting them on a pan in the freezer until just firm and then packaging them for long term storage. Usually done with fragile foods.

Fold: Folding is done when a substance that has a lot of air in it, like whipped cream or beaten egg whites, is mixed into a heavier ingredient, like a batter. A rubber spatula or large spoon can be used to carefully lift and mix.

Grate: This usually means to rub a solid food, like vegetables or cheese against a grater. A grater has sharp blades that cut the solid food into smaller pieces.

Marinate: This means to cover food in a seasoned liquid that contains some form of acid, like fruit juice, wine, or vinegar. This is done to tenderize and flavor a food.

Mince: This means to chop very, very fine.

Pinch: As a measurement, it is a very small amount. What you can hold between your thumb and index finger.

Puree: This means to mash something until it is a uniformly smooth product. This is done with a blender, food processor, or food mill.

Reduce: Boil or simmer a liquid to reduce its volume and intensify its flavor.

Sauté: This is a slower form of frying, requiring lower heat and less fat.

Simmer: Simmering is a *very* slow boil. The bubbles should barely break the surface of the liquid.

Steam: This means to cook or heat food over boiling water, with the food not touching the water. This is a very healthy way to cook. Usually uses a steamer basket inside a pan and a lid.

Stock: This is an intensely flavored broth. The liquid is simmered until much of it evaporates, leaving a stronger flavored product.

Whisk: This means to beat with a whisk or whip until the food is well mixed.

Freezer Selection & Maintenance

Whether you are considering purchasing a brand-new freezer, or looking for a reliable used model, there are a few important things to consider. Plan to purchase your appliance from a dealer who services what he sells. Look for a well-known brand so that parts are not hard to find for repairs. If your freezer is new, fill out the warranty card and send it in to the manufacturer right away. Keep the Owner's Manual!

Construction

A freezer cabinet should be made of a wrap-around, one-piece structure. The compressor should be hermetically sealed so that it requires no maintenance from you. It should have leveling feet on the cabinet. The controls should be positioned so that *you* can reach them easily, but toddlers can't. Freezer door seals are usually magnetic. Make sure that the seal is tight on all edges. If you close a piece of paper in the door it should be held tightly. If you have children, you might consider purchasing a freezer with a built-in lock. This will prevent food from "disappearing" and more importantly, will prevent the freezer door from being left open "accidentally".

"Frost-Free" vs. "Frost-Full"

Defrosting is a burdensome chore for most homeowners. Frost-free models eliminate the problem by utilizing small heaters that melt the ice periodically. Because of the drying action and heat, it is especially important to properly package food headed for a frost-free appliance. Frost-free models cost around 50% more to operate than standard freezers. They are also more expensive to purchase. Because it costs more to operate and to purchase a frost-free model, you will have to determine if the cost is worth it. Most people only have to defrost a freezer once or twice a year. Look for the Federal Trade Commission (FTC) label on the appliance. The label will tell you how many kilowatt-hours the appliance will use. The smaller the number listed, the less energy is used. You should never run a frost-free freezer in a place where the temperature goes below 60°F. The compressor will not be turned on enough to keep the food from thawing.

Capacity

Check the capacity of the freezer and buy the size that is most suited to your eating patterns. A nearly full freezer runs much more efficiently than a half full one. If you purchase a freezer that is too large for your use, it may have a lot of air space that you have to cool. The freezer has to work harder to keep air cool than food, so frozen air takes more energy than frozen food!

Upright Freezers

Uprights range in size from 12 to 30 cu ft. A sliding basket or drawer is very handy for bulky items. Some come with ice makers, but they are usually optional, and they do take up room. A benefit of upright freezers is that they take up less floor space than a chest freezer of the same capacity. Also, the food is easily stacked and distributed on the shelves, and it is easier to find what you need without digging. This is a great benefit for the shorter folks among us! The temperature in the door storage spaces will be a bit warmer than the temperature in the back.

Chest Freezers

The sizes for these models run from 5 to 28 cu. ft. They generally cost less to buy than upright models. You also have more useable space in a chest freezer, because you can pack it clear to the top if you like. Utilizing baskets or boxes can help keep foods organized. Chest freezers are also more cost efficient to operate. The frozen food is packed more tightly together, so it holds the chill in. Also, since heat rises, opening the lid of a chest freezer allows less cold air to escape than opening the door of an upright freezer. In a chest freezer, the top center section will generally be a little warmer than the rest of the freezer.

Chest Freezers are very efficient and hold more than you think!

Continued on Page 136

Installment

Most people do not have the luxury of a large freezer in or near the kitchen. The room it takes up is a big consideration for where to place a freezer. Also, you want to make sure you don't have it in a spot that is too warm or too cold. If your freezer is in the kitchen, it will have to work harder because of the surrounding temperature. Any spot that is relatively cool, out of direct sunlight, dry, and well ventilated is a suitable one for a freezer. The freezer will actually run better if it is in a room that remains above 40°F. Think about where you will plug it in. A freezer should be plugged into its own, grounded outlet. A freezer should also have its own circuit so that an overload from another appliance does not shut it off. The outlet should be in a position that it is as protected as possible. No one (pets included) should be able to become tangled in the cord. An unseen pulled plug spells disaster for your frozen foods! You should not push a freezer tightly up against a wall, or into a corner. A freezer needs room to dispel heat into the air. It is a very good idea to decide *where* the freezer will go, before you decide on a size or type. It is a good idea to set the leveling feet so that it tips back slightly. This will cause the door to swing shut automatically.

Temperature Settings

0°F is a temperature that will keep the foods you store well protected. Even though water freezes at 32°F, destructive enzymes are not kept from harming your foods at that temperature. The lower the temperature, the longer the food will store well. A temperature of -5°F will keep quality even longer, but be aware that your electric bill will rise as the temperature lowers!

If you will be away from home for more than a couple of days, have a neighbor or friend check up on your freezer to make sure it is still running. Tara left on her honeymoon only to return to a defrosted chest freezer and soggy remains of her wedding cake!

Defrosting

Follow the manufacturer's instructions (if you have them) for defrosting or do a web search for "freezer defrosting". If your freezer is running well and the seal is in good shape, you should not have to defrost more than once or twice a year. You should defrost before the ice is 1/2" thick on the interior walls. This job will take anywhere from 2 to 3 hours, so allow plenty of time.

Here is a method that will work in the absence of the original manufacturer's instructions.

1. Plan to defrost your freezer at a time when it is fairly empty already.
2. For an extra safety precaution, wear rubber-soled shoes to keep you from sliding across the floor or from getting an electrical shock.
3. Remove the frozen food and place it in coolers, or wrap the food containers in several sheets of newsprint and pack it tightly into cardboard boxes or crates.
4. You need to shut off the power to the freezer, or unplug the appliance.
5. If you are working on a chest freezer, be sure to prop the lid open so that it can't come crashing down.
6. Place some old towels on the floor in front of the freezer and a rolled up towel on the bottom of an upright freezer next to the rubber door seal. This will keep water from pouring out the bottom.
7. Clean the freezer as quickly as possible. Some manufacturers say to place pans of hot water in the freezer and close the door. Then, remove the frost as it loosens and replace the water as it cools. Make sure the freezer is completely cool before restarting it. Other manufacturers do not recommend using pans of hot water in their freezers because the refrigerant pressure could build up in the evaporator, making restarting the freezer difficult. These manufacturers recommend allowing the frost to thaw naturally or with the aid of a fan.
8. You can also use a rag dipped in very hot water to drench and melt the ice. A bulb baster works well too. Draw boiling hot water into it, then squirt it over the ice. Just be very careful not to burn yourself. Repeat the hot water drenching until you are down to the bare surface.
9. If your freezer has a drip tray underneath it, empty it every once in a while to keep it from overflowing. If you need to, sop up the melted ice with a rag or sponge and squeeze the water into a bucket or tub.
10. Do not use an ice pick, screwdriver, hammer, or knife to break apart the ice. Besides the danger to yourself, you will probably damage the inside of your freezer! You might just mark up the inside, or you might even break right through a coolant line, which will release toxic fumes into the air and kill your freezer.
11. Dry out the compartment with a clean dry towel.

Exterior Cleaning

When you are finished defrosting a freezer, it is a great time to clean and deodorize it also. If you can, drag the whole appliance away from the wall. Vacuum up the dirt and mop up the remaining grime. Remove the grate in the back that covers the compressor and fan. This is usually at the very top, or very bottom of the appliance. Use a vacuum cleaner with a nozzle attachment to remove the accumulated dust around the compressor and fan. Replace the cover. Use an all-purpose cleaner to safely clean the outside of the freezer. Vacuum the dust off the condenser coils. When you are done and everything is clean and dry, turn the power to the freezer back on or plug it back into its outlet. Turn the freezer back on and make sure the temperature control is set where you want it to be. Wait 15-30 minutes to allow the freezer to become chilled before returning the food to the freezer. If food packages are frosty, scrape or wipe them to remove frost or moisture.

Interior Cleaning

For food residues, use a paste made of baking soda and water. Use it like a scouring powder to scrub the food off. Rinse the baking soda mixture off with clean warm water and a sponge or a rag. A baking soda and water solution is also a good rinse for the entire freezer. Besides the cleaning it will get, the baking soda also helps to remove odors.

Stubborn Odors

If there are stubborn odors in the freezer that the baking soda did not remove, try these options one at a time so that there will not be any chemical reactions between them. Rinse out the freezer with clear water if needed and wipe it dry before trying another method.

1. Vinegar and water solution - mix one cup of vinegar with one gallon of water.
2. Household chlorine bleach - mix a half cup of bleach with one gallon of water.
3. Leave crumpled up black and white newsprint in the freezer with the door shut.
4. Place charcoal briquettes in a tub or pan and leave them in the freezer with the door shut.
5. Make a mild solution of dish washing liquid and water. Wash with the mixture, then rinse with clean water.

Sometimes the odor is impossible to remove. Food that has been in the freezer too long, food that has been improperly packaged, or food that has spoiled in a power outage can cause lasting odors. If smelly moisture is absorbed by the freezer insulation, it may have strong permanent odors. You can either have the insulation replaced by an appliance repairman, or live with the problem. If you choose to put up with the odor, try to double wrap all of the foods in the freezer. When you take the food from the freezer, discard the outer wrapper. Hopefully *it* will contain the odor, not the inner wrap and food beneath it.

There are 60+ entrees in this upright freezer. Don't you wish they were yours?

Power Failure!

It's happened to all of us! The storm comes through and we lose power the day AFTER we stocked our freezer. Or worse yet, we run down to the basement and discover that "someone" has left the freezer door open. What do we do? Is the food safe? Does everything need to be thrown away "just to be sure"?

The following information comes from the USDA. One idea that they didn't offer (probably because they don't have kids) is to use the lock and key that most likely came built into your freezer. This will keep your kids from eating 20 popsicles in one day and "accidentally" leaving the door open.

In the event of a power outage, freezer failure or open freezer door, the food may still be safe to use. Without power, a full upright or chest freezer will keep everything frozen for about 2 days. A half-full freezer will keep food frozen 1 day. If the power will be coming back on fairly soon, you can make the food last longer by keeping the door shut as much as possible and covering the unit with blankets and quilts. Make sure that you do not block the air vent. If the freezer is not full, quickly group packages together so they will retain the cold more effectively. Separate meat and poultry items from other foods so that if they begin to thaw, their juices won't drip onto other foods.

For short term power outages – less than 6 hours – just leave the door closed until the power returns. If the power is off for more than 6 hours, you may want to put block ice or bags of ice in the freezer or transfer foods to a friend's freezer until power is restored. Use an appliance thermometer to monitor the temperature.

To determine the safety of foods when the power goes on (or you first discover the open door), check their condition and temperature. If food is partly frozen, still has ice crystals or is as cold as if it were in a refrigerator (40 degrees), it is safe to refreeze or use. It is not necessary to cook raw foods before refreezing (see tips below). Discard foods that have been warmer than 40 degrees for more than two hours. Discard any foods that have been contaminated by raw meat juices. Dispose of soft or melted ice cream for quality's sake.

Without power, a refrigerator will keep food cool for 4-6 hours depending on the kitchen temperature. A full, well-functioning freezer unit above a refrigerator should keep food frozen for 2 days. A half full one will keep food frozen for about 1 day. If you have access to it, block ice can keep food on the refrigerator shelves cooler.

Re-freezing Foods

As a general rule, if the power has been off for quite a while, and then comes back on, food still containing ice crystals or that feel refrigerator-cold can be refrozen. Do not be surprised if a little quality is lost in re-freezing. Discard any thawed food that has risen to room temperature and remained so two hours or more. Immediately throw out anything with a strange color or odor. Before you begin to re-freeze food, be sure to turn the freezer to its coldest temperature. Mark the foods as "re-frozen". Space the food out on the shelves so that air can flow freely around the packages. When all the foods are solidly re-frozen, return the temperature setting to its normal position.

Meats - To re-freeze meats, re-package them in freezer bags, or tightly sealed rigid freezer containers. Do not refreeze ground meats that have thawed. Only re-freeze ground meat packages that are still solidly frozen. Icy cold packages of thawed meat can be cooked thoroughly, then re-packaged for the freezer.

Cured Meats - Ham, bacon, hard salami, and pepperoni can be re-frozen if they are still cold to the touch.

Poultry – Re-package icy poultry in moisture-vapor proof packaging before re-freezing. Leave the original wrapping on it, but place it inside a freezer bag or rigid freezer container. Discard any poultry that has come to room temperature. If poultry juices have dripped onto other foods, treat them like thawed poultry - throw them out! If the poultry is still cold, cook and eat it right away, or cook it and freeze immediately.

Fish - Do not re-freeze fish unless it is still solidly frozen. If the fish is thawed, but very cold to the touch, cook it and consume immediately. Throw out any fish that has come to room temperature.

Fruits - Use thawed fruits to make jams, jellies, preserves, or cooked pie fillings.

Vegetables - You can re-freeze vegetables that still have ice crystals in them. If the vegetables are thawed but still in good condition, you can cook and eat them.

Miscellaneous - Completely thawed baked goods, dinner entrees, juices and cheese should not be re-frozen. If they are still cold, they should be refrigerated and eaten as soon as possible. Do not eat dinner entrees that have thawed to room temperature.

Nutritional Information for "Lite" Recipes

Lazy Day Lasagna - Lite
Replace cottage cheese with low fat cottage cheese, mozzarella with low fat mozzarella. Used a meatless spaghetti sauce for the nutritional analysis.
Per Serving: 214 Calories; 7g Fat (29.3% calories from fat); 12g Protein; 25g Carbohydrate; 2g Dietary Fiber; 40mg Cholesterol; 605mg Sodium.
Exchanges: 1-1/2 Grain (Starch); 1 Lean Meat; 1 Fat; 1/2 Other Carbohydrates.

Parsley Parmesan Chicken - Lite
Replace Italian salad dressing with fat free Italian Salad dressing and fryer part with 6 chicken breast halves.
Per Serving: 191 Calories; 4g Fat (18.9% of calories); 31g Protein; 6g Carbohydrate; trace Fiber; 74mg Cholesterol; 592mg Sodium.
Exchanges: 1/2 Grain(Starch); 4 Lean Meat.

Crispy Rice Chicken - Lite
Replaced fresh fryer parts with chicken breast.
Per Serving: 169 Calories; 2g Fat (12.5% of calories); 29g Protein; 7g Carbohydrate; trace Fiber; 100mg Cholesterol; 316mg Sodium.
Exchanges: 1/2 Grain(Starch); 4 Lean Meat; 0 Fat.

Italian Chicken - Lite
Replace dressing with fat free dressing, cream cheese with light cream cheese and cream of chicken soup with reduced fat cream of chicken soup.
Per Serving: 280 Calories; 9g Fat (31.8% of calories); 34g Protein; 12g Carbohydrate; 1g Fiber; 94mg Cholesterol; 1551mg Sodium.
Exchanges: 4-1/2 Lean Meat; 1 Fat.

Baked Chicken Fingers & Nuggets Sauce #1 - Lite
Replace mayonnaise with a light version and 2% milk with skim milk.
Per Serving: 267 Calories; 6g Fat (19.6% of calories); 37g Protein; 15g Carbohydrate; 1g Fiber; 97mg Cholesterol; 291mg Sodium.
Exchanges: 1 Grain(Starch); 4-1/2 Lean Meat; 1/2 Fat.

Baked Chicken Fingers & Nuggets Sauce #2 - Lite
Replace 2% milk with skim milk and ranch dressing with reduced-calorie ranch dressing.
Per Serving: 274 Calories; 7g Fat (23.6% of calories); 36g Protein; 14g Carbohydrate; trace Fiber; 92mg Cholesterol; 327mg Sodium.
Exchanges: 1 Grain(Starch); 4-1/2 Lean Meat; 1/2 Fat.

Seafood Lasagna - Lite
Replace 2% milk with skim milk, Swiss cheese with low fat Swiss cheese.
Per Serving: 439 Calories; 6g Fat (13.2% of calories); 21g Protein; 72g Carbohydrate; 3g Fiber; 29mg Cholesterol; 356mg Sodium.
Exchanges: 4-1/2 Grain(Starch); 1 Lean Meat; 1/2 Vegetable; 1/2 Fat.

Cheese-Filled Shells - Lite
Replace cottage cheese with low fat cottage cheese and mozzarella cheese with reduced fat mozzarella cheese.
Per Serving: 607 Calories; 16g Fat (23.5% of calories); 36g Protein; 77g Carbohydrate; 4g Fiber; 81mg Cholesterol; 1593mg Sodium.
Exchanges: 3-1/2 Grain(Starch); 3-1/2 Lean Meat; 1-1/2 Fat; 1 Other Carbohydrates.

Tex-Mex Lasagna - Lite
Replace ricotta cheese with low fat ricotta cheese.
Per Serving: 479 Calories; 6g Fat (12.1% of calories); 23g Protein; 82g Carbohydrate; 6g Fiber; 18mg Cholesterol; 565mg Sodium.
Exchanges: 5-1/2 Grain(Starch); 1-1/2 Lean Meat; 1/2 Fat.

Pasta with Herb Sauce - Lite
Replace 2% milk with skim milk and ricotta with reduced fat ricotta.
Per Serving: 136 Calories; 2g Fat (13.1% of calories); 7g Protein; 23g Carbohydrate; 1g Fiber; 6mg Cholesterol; 282mg Sodium.
Exchanges: 1-1/2 Grain(Starch); 1/2 Lean Meat.

Spicy Tofu Enchiladas - Lite
Replace cheddar cheese with low fat cheddar cheese.
Per Serving: 381 Calories; 15g Fat (33.1% of calories); 19g Protein; 47g Carbohydrate; 10g Fiber; 27mg Cholesterol; 827mg Sodium.
Exchanges: 3 Grain(Starch); 2-1/2 Lean Meat; 1-1/2 Vegetable; 2 Fat.

Breakfast Egg Casserole - Lite
Replaced cheddar cheese with low fat cheddar cheese and 2% milk with skim milk.
Per Serving: 275 Calories; 12g Fat (40.0% of calories); 20g Protein; 20g Carbohydrate; 1g Fiber; 127mg Cholesterol; 819mg Sodium.
Exchanges: 1 Grain(Starch); 2 Lean Meat; 1 Fat.

Beefy Vegetable Soup - Lite
Replace ground round with ground turkey. Make thickener without the margarine as you would make a fat free white sauce.
Per Serving: 292 Calories; 10g Fat (30.1% of calories); 31g Protein; 21g Carbohydrate; 4g Fiber; 90mg Cholesterol; 2023mg Sodium.
Exchanges: 3-1/2 Lean Meat; 2-1/2 Vegetable.

Cheddar Broccoli Soup - Lite
Replace 2% milk with skim milk and cheddar cheese with low fat cheddar cheese.
Per Serving: 250 Calories; 13g Fat (47.0% of calories); 16g Protein; 18g Carbohydrate; 3g Fiber; 9mg Cholesterol; 447mg Sodium.
Exchanges: 1/2 Grain(Starch); 1-1/2 Lean Meat; 1 Vegetable; 1/2 Non-Fat Milk; 2 Fat.

Taco Chili - Lite
Replace ground round with ground turkey, sour cream with light sour cream and cheddar cheese with low fat cheddar cheese.
Per Serving: 429 Calories; 17g Fat (35.7% of calories); 24g Protein; 46g Carbohydrate; 9g Fiber; 63mg Cholesterol; 1080mg Sodium.
Exchanges: 2-1/2 Grain(Starch); 2-1/2 Lean Meat; 1 Vegetable; 2 Fat.

INDEX

Index continued...

Index continued...

■ T ■

■ V ■

■ W ■

Customer Order Form

(Use this form to order any of our products or visit us on the web at www.30daygourmet.com/store to place your order online)

Customer's Name		Today's Date

Address	City	State	Zip

Home Phone	Work Phone	E-mail Address

Quantity	Description	Price Each	Total
	Freezer Cooking Manual	$14.95	
	"30 Day Gourmet " Logo Apron	$19.95	
	Freezer Labels – pkg. of 50	$4.00	
	Advantage Cooking Software	$34.95	
	Cook's Assistant Notebook	$12.95	
	Sheet Protectors - pkg. of 50	$6.00	
	Kitchen Pro Calculator – desktop	$34.95	
	Kitchen Calculator – handheld	$24.95	
	"30 Day Gourmet Live" Video	$19.95	
	eBook CD – Holiday Freezer Cooking	$8.95	
	eBook CD – Freezer Cooking on a Budget	$8.95	
	eBook CD – Freezer Lunches To Go	$8.95	
	eBook CD – Freezer Desserts to Die For!	$8.95	
	eBook CD – Freezer Cooking for Daycare Providers and Busy Parents	$8.95	
	eBook CD - Healthy Meals Freezer Cooking	$8.85	
	eBook CD - Co-op Cuisine	$8.95	

Shipping Charges		Total		Sub	$
Up to $23.95	$5.00			+Shipping	$
$24.00-$35.95	$6.00			+6% tax(IN only)	$
$36.00-$49.95	$7.00			TOTAL	$
Over $50.00	FREE		Method of Payment:		
			____ Check (enclosed)		
			____ Credit Card # _____ - _____ - _____ - _____		
			Exp. Date _____/_____ Name on card: _____		

Prices subject to change without notice.

30 Day Gourmet ■ **P.O. Box 272** ■ **Brownsburg, IN 46112**